# THE PARTY

A Play in Two Acts

by Jane Arden

## SAMUEL FRENCH

ISBN 978-0-573-01330-0

www.concordtheatricals.co.uk
www.concordtheatricals.com

---

**FOR AMATEUR PRODUCTION ENQUIRIES**

UNITED KINGDOM AND WORLD
EXCLUDING NORTH AMERICA
licensing@concordtheatricals.co.uk
020-7054-7200

UNITED STATES AND CANADA
Info@concordtheatricals.com
1-866-979-0447

Each title is subject to availability from Concord Theatricals,
depending upon country of performance.

---

This work is published by Samuel French Ltd, an imprint of Concord Theatricals.

The professional rights in this play are controlled by Concord Theatricals, Aldwych House, 71-91 Aldwych, London WC2B 4HN.

## MUSIC USE NOTE

## IMPORTANT BILLING AND CREDIT REQUIREMENTS

## THE PARTY

*THE PARTY* was produced at the New Theatre, London, on the 28th May 1958. It was directed by Charles Laughton with settings by Reece Pemberton. The cast was as follows:

| | |
|---|---|
| HENRIETTA BROUGH | Ann Lynn |
| FRANCES BROUGH, her mother | Joyce Redman |
| HAROLD LINGHAM, the paying guest | John Welsh |
| ELSIE SHARP | Elsa Lanchester |
| SOYA MARSHALL | Albert Finney |
| RICHARD BROUGH, Henrietta's father | Charles Laughton |

# CHARACTERS

**HENRIETTA BROUGH**
**FRANCES BROUGH**
**HAROLD LINGHAM**
**ELSIE SHARP**
**SOYA MARSHALL**
**RICHARD BROUGH**

# SETTING

The action of the play passes in the living room of the Broughs' home in Kilburn, London.

# TIME

The present.

## ACT I

**Scene One**   Late afternoon on a Friday in early spring
**Scene Two**   Later the same evening
**Scene Three**   Two days later. 5.30 p.m.

## ACT II

**Scene One**   Later the same evening
**Scene Two**   Early the following morning

# ACT I

## Scene One

*Scene – the living room of the **BROUGHS'** home in Kilburn, London. Late afternoon on a Friday in early spring.*

*It is an ugly room, aggressively uncomfortable in its architecture, part of an old Victorian house. We sense immediately that, adjoining the room, are dark passages which demand the electric light even on the sunniest day. It is a room which no matter how hard you scrub it, never looks really clean. There is a deep fireplace back centre, with built-in chimney corner seats, and through the angular bay windows right and left of the fireplace, we can see and hear the sounds of a lively working-class shopping area. The entrance hall up right is open to the room, with the front door right of the back wall and a door to the kitchen up right. The room is dominated by the dark, narrow, linoleum-covered staircase which leads up from the hall to the other floor of the maisonette. A door left leads to **LINGHAM**'s room. There has been an attempt to create femininity over the upright masculine lines of the room; homemade chintz covers, floral prints on the wall. In spite of this the fight for cosiness has been lost. This is a room for moles who hide away in the darkness of their defeat. A large sofa stands right of the fireplace with an armchair opposite. A stool stands in front of the fireplace between the sofa and armchair. There is a dining table right with benches right and left of it and an armchair at the upstage end. A long, low chest is down centre. Shelves for books are built-in around the door left. A telephone*

*stands on an extension of the shelves down left. At night the
room is lit by wall-brackets right and left and an electric
pendant in the hall, with switches at the foot of the stairs.*

*When the curtain rises, the lights are on, but the window
curtains are not yet drawn.* **HENRIETTA BROUGH** *is seated
in the armchair left centre, speaking on the telephone. She
is a girl in the throes of adolescence; a girl with grace and
charm but, as yet, no compassion. Her great struggle is
for control and how to fit the pattern of everyday into her
virulent imagination. She is easily hurt and hurts easily
and, at the moment, loves only that which is beautiful.*

**HENRIETTA** *(into the telephone)* Yes, about twenty... No, I haven't
asked Kenny and Martin yet... You know Margaret... No,
beautiful... Vulgar? Oh, no. Terribly modern, of course.

**FRANCES BROUGH** *enters by the front door and goes to
the upstage end of the table. She is a passive and gentle
woman of thirty-nine, and is the woman who gives herself
to one person and makes no terms. Love for her is a simple
matter and only when to love simply is impossible, does
conflict arise in her life. Her appeal is all softness and no
judgement. She is wearing her outdoor clothes and carries
a string bag of shopping, a bucket bag and her handbag.*

Did you notice those tiny bits of hair at the back of her neck,
how they fall into place? ...

**FRANCES** *puts her bags on the upstage end of the table.*

No, God just made it happen... You wouldn't think he'd be so
prejudiced in favour of such an awful girl...

**FRANCES** Ettie, don't talk about God like that. *(She removes her
gloves and coat.)*

**HENRIETTA** I just said how nice it was of him to have managed
Margaret's head so well.

**FRANCES** Well, talk gently, dear. *(She hangs her coat on the hooks
in the hall.)*

HENRIETTA *(into the telephone)* I'm speaking to Mother... *(her voice becomes tense)* Father? ...No, he's still away... Oh, I never write. Letters are just a blank to me...

FRANCES *takes a vacuum flask from the bucket bag, puts it on the table, then picks up the bucket bag and moves to the right-hand fireside seat.*

Oh, he's getting better... *(she turns to* FRANCES*)* Give me the party list off the mantelpiece, will you?

FRANCES *takes a list from the mantelpiece, crosses and gives it to* HENRIETTA.

FRANCES Talk about something else, be a good girl. *(She hugs* HENRIETTA.*)*

HENRIETTA *(anxiously)* The party's still on, isn't it?

FRANCES *(moving to the right-hand fireside seat)* Of course, but just don't ramble on so.

*She opens the right-hand fireside seat, takes two office files from the bucket bag, puts them in the seat box, takes some raffia work and coloured raffia from the box and puts it in the bag.*

HENRIETTA Well, there are so many things to do. Sunday's almost here. *(into the telephone)* I haven't quite completed the list, yet... I got the white one... Oh, no, it's sacred for Sunday. *(She turns to* FRANCES.*)* Did the dress arrive yet?

FRANCES *(moving to the hall)* No, dear. *(She puts the bucket bag in the hall with her coat then moves to the table.)*

HENRIETTA *(desperately)* Supposing it doesn't come?

FRANCES It'll come. *(She collects the vacuum flask and string bag from the table.)*

HENRIETTA Oh, you're so cosy. It *must* come. Nothing goes wrong when you say so.

FRANCES *exits to the kitchen.*

*(into the telephone)* Well, there is one thing you can do if you don't mind... Do you know Soya Marshall? ...You do? ...How well? Enough to invite him? ...You will? ...You promise? ...Absolutely? ...Will you do it now? ...Well, there isn't much time – it's Friday today and the party's Sunday... *(her face drops)* Supposing he's busy? ...Well, call me back... *(casually)* Of course not, but he looks passable and he'll make up the number. Do you think he'll bring anyone? ...Oh, yes, ask him just the same...

FRANCES *enters from the kitchen, carrying a tray with plates, knives, tablecloth, etc. She puts the tray on the bench left of the table, then crosses to the window up left and closes the curtains.*

No, I'm not actually seventeen until next Wednesday, but I'm having it early because my father's coming home... Oh, no, he *hates* parties... Yes, I met Soya once but he wouldn't remember. *(dreamily)* He was wearing a *wonderful* suede jacket...

FRANCES *crosses to the window up right and closes the curtains.*

Well, good-bye... You will call me back? ... 'Bye.

*She rises, replaces the receiver, moves down left and puts the telephone on the bookshelves.*

FRANCES You mustn't think so much about what people wear, Ettie.

HENRIETTA *(moving to the fireplace)* But it's important. *(She puts the party list on the mantelpiece.)* I'm sure his socks are really beautiful.

FRANCES *(moving to the upstage end of the table)* Please, Ettie!

HENRIETTA *(continuing)* And his room, and his books, smooth, clean, really in control. *(She turns to* FRANCES.*)* You know.

FRANCES *smiles, transfers her handbag to the bench left of the table and during the following speeches, lays the table.*

FRANCES Yes, I know.

HENRIETTA *(moving to the bench left of the table)* Mother, he wouldn't bring anyone, would he? *(She sits on the bench, facing front.)*

FRANCES No, I'm sure not.

HENRIETTA But if he *does*?

FRANCES If he does, we can get to know him later.

HENRIETTA *(sharply)* No, it *must* be Sunday.

FRANCES *(looking into HENRIETTA's face)* Before your father comes home? *(She pauses. With a change of tone:)* Don't set your heart on this boy coming. Have you spoken to him?

HENRIETTA No, but I've looked and looked. You have only to look.

FRANCES And you can see underneath the suede jacket?

HENRIETTA Mother!

FRANCES Ettie, I didn't mean it like that.

HENRIETTA I'm so happy – so delirious.

FRANCES Well, supposing he doesn't come?

HENRIETTA *(horrified)* What will I do with all the others?

FRANCES You mean the rest of the guests?

HENRIETTA *(rising)* Oh, they're just background. *(She pauses and moves centre. Tentatively:)* When will Father be home?

FRANCES Quite soon now. *(She picks up her handbag and takes out a letter.)* I had a letter this morning. I'll read it to you.

HENRIETTA *(turning to face front)* Not before Monday? He wouldn't come Sunday?

FRANCES Ettie, why did you lie on the phone?

HENRIETTA *(moving to the armchair left centre; furtively)* Lie about what? *(She flops into the armchair and lies back in it.)*

FRANCES You implied that your father won't like to come to the birthday. *(She replaces the letter in the bag.)*

HENRIETTA I had to say something.

FRANCES There was no need to imply that.

HENRIETTA Well, what could I say?

FRANCES Nothing, I suppose.

HENRIETTA No-one will think it funny, him not being here.

FRANCES *(putting her bag on the bench right of the table.)* That's not what I care about. *(She attends to the table laying.)*

HENRIETTA *flounces up from the armchair and twirls to centre.*

HENRIETTA *(changing the subject)* Shall we make the room look absolutely beautiful? Like a fair? No, not like a fair, that's too noisy. Like a ballet.

FRANCES *(smiling reminiscently)* I went to a party once. Fancy dress. Your father was there as Robin Hood.

HENRIETTA How funny.

FRANCES No, he won first prize.

HENRIETTA What were you? I bet you were Cleopatra.

FRANCES I've got a photo of him somewhere, getting the prize.

HENRIETTA Oh, don't get those old pictures out now.

FRANCES *(moving to the chest down centre)* I remember now. They're in this chest – in a most terrible muddle. I've always meant to clear it out. *(She turns to HENRIETTA.)* Where's the key?

HENRIETTA Must you look at them now?

FRANCES I'd like to, Ettie.

HENRIETTA It's in the blue vase.

FRANCES *(moving to the fireplace)* How did it get there? *(She turns and looks at HENRIETTA.)*

**HENRIETTA** I put it there. I cleared out the chest. *(She is bordering on hysteria.)* One day I couldn't stand the mess anymore so I just turned it out.

**FRANCES** Then you came across the picture?

**HENRIETTA** I don't remember. *(She turns defiantly to* **FRANCES**.*)* I really don't remember.

**FRANCES** But they were giving him the prize.

**HENRIETTA** *turns away left centre.*

*(she moves to the stool and sits, facing front)* You must remember. The feather in his hat hides my face. You must remember, Ettie – it hides my face – the feather...

**HENRIETTA** *(with set face)* I burned it.

**FRANCES** You burned it?

**HENRIETTA** I burnt a lot of pictures. You said you were going to, and I didn't think that one was important. *(She tries to justify herself.)* It looked so silly and I couldn't see your face, so I burned it. I didn't think it mattered.

**FRANCES** That was the night your father proposed to me.

**HENRIETTA** *(near to tears)* I'm sorry but I didn't think it was important.

**FRANCES** There was a Chinese lantern in the corner of the picture. Did you see it?

**HENRIETTA** No. I didn't look very hard.

**FRANCES** Didn't you see how happy he looked?

**HENRIETTA** *(turning and kneeling beside* **FRANCES***)* I'm sorry I've hurt you.

**FRANCES** That doesn't matter. *(She puts her arm around* **HENRIETTA** *and takes her hand.)* But didn't you see how *happy* he looked? *(She tries to catch* **HENRIETTA** *at a weak moment.)* Ettie, let me phone your father and tell him you're having a party and ask him to come home.

**HENRIETTA** *(back on her guard)* No.

**FRANCES** We could put up Chinese lanterns.

**HENRIETTA** I'm sorry I've hurt you.

**FRANCES** Let me *ask* him, Ettie.

**HENRIETTA** No. *(She rises and turns away.)*

> **FRANCES** *retains hold of* **HENRIETTA**'*s hand.*

**FRANCES** *(pleading)* Wouldn't it be nice as a homecoming. Your father and I wouldn't stay the whole time at the party. After all, we'd want to talk.

> **HENRIETTA** *tries to free her hand.*

But wouldn't it be nice?

> **HENRIETTA** *breaks away and leans on the downstage arm of the armchair left centre, facing front.*

**HENRIETTA** *(thinking up excuses)* I think it would be nicer for Father to come on a day that's just for him. You know, a special tea. With all those people, he wouldn't be comfortable.

**FRANCES** *(rising and taking a step towards* **HENRIETTA**.*)* You mean, *you* wouldn't be comfortable. What are you going to do with him after Sunday, Ettie?

**HENRIETTA** *Do* with him?

**FRANCES** Where are you going to hide him? Where are you going to hide him after Sunday, Ettie?

> **HAROLD LINGHAM** *enters by the front door. He is a painfully introverted man, aged fifty-seven. He is a Civil Servant and a bachelor, the paying guest at the Broughs'. He is carrying a dress box and a parcel of laundry.* **FRANCES** *moves above the table.*

**LINGHAM** *(closing the door)* Good evening, Mrs. Brough. *(He hangs his hat on the hook in the hall.)* Good evening, Henrietta. *(He comes into the room, and puts the laundry parcel on the sofa.)*

The postman just gave me this parcel. *(He indicates the dress box.)* It looks such an exciting shape. It's for you, Henrietta. *(He reads the label.)* "Miss Brough".

HENRIETTA *crosses, takes the box from* LINGHAM, *sits on the left-hand fireside seat and hugs the box.* FRANCES *picks up her empty tray.*

How the time goes on. It's such a fresh day. Spring's coming on, I'm sure. I walked home the long way, and managed to collect the laundry.

*During the following speeches he transfers the laundry to the chest down right, opens the parcel, takes out the laundry book and puts it beside the parcel on the chest.*

FRANCES How much do I owe you?

LINGHAM I'll deduct it from what I owe for the room. It's two weeks, I think, and six and six for the hyacinth you so kindly bought.

FRANCES Aren't you going to open your parcel, Henrietta?

HENRIETTA No, later.

LINGHAM No doubt it's something for the celebrations.

HENRIETTA It's my dress.

LINGHAM What a wonderful time for your father to be coming home.

HENRIETTA *(rising and moving below the sofa)* I'll look at my dress in my room.

FRANCES *(intercepting* HENRIETTA*)* No, stay here. I'll get some tea. I bought crumpets.

HENRIETTA I'm not hungry.

FRANCES *(firmly)* Show Mr. Lingham the dress while I get the tea.

HENRIETTA All right, but I'm sure he's not interested in dresses.

FRANCES *exits to the kitchen.* LINGHAM *removes his coat, crosses and hangs it in the hall.*

LINGHAM  Well, I'm not an expert, of course, but I must admit I'm curious.

HENRIETTA  All right, I'll show you. *(She opens the box and a white dress falls to the floor.)*

LINGHAM  *(picking up the dress; very gently)* What a wonderful time for your father to be coming home.

HENRIETTA  *(determined to cut him short)* Father isn't coming to the party. *(She moves to the armchair left centre and sits.)*

LINGHAM  *(not understanding)* Not coming?

HENRIETTA  Well, what's so strange about that?

LINGHAM  *(dazed)* Not coming?

HENRIETTA  He's been away for three months. Why should he be getting back just for my party? It's just an old party. Anyway, it's *my* birthday.

LINGHAM  *(completely bewildered)* Of course, but I thought he was coming home this weekend.

HENRIETTA  *(speaking very quickly; trying to explain everything away)* Oh, no – Monday, perhaps Tuesday. *(She rises and moves to left of* LINGHAM.*)* We're going to have a special tea and you must be there. You *will* be there?

LINGHAM  Of course – a special tea. *(He hands the dress to* HENRIETTA.*)* Careful with your beautiful dress. *(He crosses to the door left.)*

HENRIETTA  You do like it.

LINGHAM *exits left, leaving the door open.*

*(she calls after him)* White is wonderful, isn't it? *(she frowns)* Mother didn't wear white at her wedding.

LINGHAM *appears in the doorway left.*

**LINGHAM** Does your father know there *is* a party?

**HENRIETTA** No – Mother thought it best not to tell him. Perhaps he'd want to come and he wouldn't be happy, she's sure.

**LINGHAM** He doesn't know there *is* a party?

**HENRIETTA** *(sharply)* I just told you, having been away so long he'll need to settle down for awhile.

*LINGHAM exits, leaving the door open.*

*She moves below the armchair left centre and leans on the downstage arm.*

*(with a change of tone)* He loves to play draughts with you. I suppose he's spent more time in your room than anywhere else in the house.

**LINGHAM** *(offstage)* I suppose he did.

**HENRIETTA** *(remembering)* All day long he'd be in your room while you were out. I often wondered what a grown man should find to do all day in that room.

*LINGHAM enters left.*

**LINGHAM** Why didn't you ask him?

**HENRIETTA** Oh, don't be silly. That was during the holidays while Mother was working at the summer show. I'd be here all day and he'd be in that room. It was most horribly quiet – a big silence. *(Suddenly)* You'll be coming in for a drink on Sunday.

**LINGHAM** No, I don't think so. Not if your father won't be there.

**HENRIETTA** *(hurt and angry)* It's *my* birthday. Don't you want to come just because it's *my* birthday?

**LINGHAM** I didn't mean to be impolite about it.

**HENRIETTA** Everyone seems to care just about Father. Father's not a child.

**LINGHAM** *(apologetically)* No, it's not that. It's just I expected him. He's been away a long time and a party is such a friendly thing. *(He crosses to the chest down centre.)* I'd better separate the laundry.

HENRIETTA *(putting the dress on the back of the armchair.)* Let me do it. *(She moves to left of* LINGHAM *and sorts the laundry.)* Six handkerchiefs, pyjamas – those are yours, aren't they? They have a little tear. I'll mend it, shall I? And shirts, two stripey ones and a white... *(She breaks off and stares at the white shirt.)*

LINGHAM Oh, that's not mine. It's your father's and – er – *(He looks at* HENRIETTA.*)* I took a small liberty – I thought he might need it. I – it's his favourite and quite crumpled so – er – I – I'm afraid I took a small liberty...

HENRIETTA You had no right.

LINGHAM Yes, I had no right. Well, I'll put it away and we'll forget about it.

HENRIETTA Why did you presume?

LINGHAM I've missed him. I've missed him coming to my room – but I had no right to presume.

HENRIETTA *(handing the white shirt to* LINGHAM; *trying to comfort him)* He can wear it when he comes – *Monday* or *Tuesday.*

LINGHAM *(not comforted)* Oh, yes, at the special tea.

HENRIETTA *(crossing above* LINGHAM *to right of him)* We'll have everything he likes – what does he like?

LINGHAM I don't know.

HENRIETTA *(crossing above* LINGHAM *to left of him)* Yes, you do. You've lived here two whole years. *(quietly)* You came here the year Father gave up law. I remember the day you moved in. *(She moves centre.)* You had tea in your room. You were shy.

LINGHAM Everything was so strange. Your father came in and sat with me. I had spilt a little milk on the cloth in my room. I was worried. I worry quite a lot about these things. It's silly, isn't it? And do you know what he said? "A lot of stupid, leaky jugs made in this world," and I felt quite all right. Such a kind man, Richard.

**HENRIETTA** I've never heard you call Father "Richard", before.

**LINGHAM** He asked me to several times. I did it once.

**HENRIETTA** When?

**LINGHAM** *(crossing towards the door left)* I can't recall.

**HENRIETTA** *(running and intercepting* **LINGHAM***)* Yes, you can. It was the night of the school dance. The first time you saw Father – *(she searches for a word)* ill.

**LINGHAM** *(moving to the chest; embarrassed)* I think I'd better clear up these things. *(He turns to* **HENRIETTA***.)* What shall I do with the shirt?

**HENRIETTA** Put it away, put it away, put it *anywhere. (She turns away up left centre.)*

**LINGHAM** Ah, yes, away – anywhere. *(He collects his laundry and turns to* **HENRIETTA***.)* Tell your mother if it's not inconvenient, I'll have tea in my room. No crumpets.

**HENRIETTA** *(turning to him)* But you *never* have tea in your room anymore.

**LINGHAM** I must write a letter. That's it, a letter to your father. I always write Fridays. Of course, this week I didn't intend to, but now I must catch the post.

**HENRIETTA** Do you call him "Richard" on paper?

**LINGHAM** No, it looks so strange. I must clear up these things. *(He moves to the armchair left centre.)*

**HENRIETTA** *(moving to right of* **LINGHAM***)* What will you say in the letter?

**LINGHAM** The usual things. There's a book on birds I've located… *(He touches the white dress on the armchair.)* This is a very nice dress.

HENRIETTA You won't mention it?

LINGHAM *(turning to her)* Mention what?

HENRIETTA Well, anything – in the letter.

LINGHAM Of course not. I would have no right to do that. *(He moves to the door left.)* Ask your mother about tea.

LINGHAM *exits left, leaving the door open.*

HENRIETTA *(calling)* Mr. Lingham, why do you always speak about Father as if he – *(she searches for a word)* were normal? *(She pauses.)*

LINGHAM *enters slowly left.*

*(she crosses and sits on the sofa.)* You were here after the dance and the Rolands' dinner. I remember you – I remember you helping and running. You and Mother looking at each other and her trembling...

LINGHAM *(moving slowly to left of the stool)* Trembling?

HENRIETTA Yes, *trembling.* Everyone trembles on occasions with Father. Sometimes, when we've been out together, he and Mother and me, I've gone into cloakrooms to stop myself shaking, or to avoid eyes watching us across a room, watching Father imitate a dog, or a bear, or a fox – it wouldn't be so bad if it were a sly fox, a fox with a purpose, but it's always a drooling fox, or a lame fox, or a fox with no tail, or no teeth, or no eyes... *(she rises)* If someone has to imitate a fox, Mr. Lingham, why at least can't it be a manly fox?

*The front door bell rings.* HENRIETTA *stands looking at* LINGHAM *for a moment then goes to the front door and opens it.* LINGHAM *moves down left.*

ELSIE SHARP *enters by the front door. She is a woman of thirty-five. No-one has ever looked after her. She is friendly and vulnerable, tactless and kind.*

ELSIE Hullo, dear. Mother about?

**HENRIETTA** She's making tea. *(She turns, goes up and sits half-way up the stairs.)*

**ELSIE** *(removing her wrap and hanging it in the hall)* Hullo, Mr. Lingham. How's city life? *(She crosses and stands below the sofa.)*

**LINGHAM** Mustn't grumble. *(He moves left centre.)* How's the nylon trade?

**ELSIE** *(moving centre; breezily)* They still run, thank the Lord. I've got a new line, now. I'm doing a bit of gents' stuff. I saw you the other day, feeding the pigeons. I was on top of a bus. Nice things, pigeons really. Eat your bread and leave you alone. *(She turns to* **HENRIETTA.***)* I hear your dad's coming home. Is he better? I did have a card last week. Sounded ever so cheerful but he didn't mention the job.

**HENRIETTA** What job?

**ELSIE** His old one, dear. At my shop. I had to take on someone else, of course, but I made it clear to the new man that it was temporary. Oh, I like having your father there. He's so quaint and always good for a laugh. This man I've got is dry as a bone.

**FRANCES** *enters from the kitchen, carrying a tray with tea, crumpets, etc.*

Hullo, Fran, how are you?

**FRANCES** *(moving to the table)* Hello, Elsie, nice to see you. *(She puts the tray on the table.)*

**ELSIE** Tea. You don't mind if I invite myself to a cup? *(She sits on the downstage arm of the sofa)*

**FRANCES** *(crossing to the chest down centre)* Of course not. *(She collects the remaining laundry.)*

**ELSIE** I dropped in because I heard Richard's coming home.

**HENRIETTA** Who told you?

**ELSIE** Old Mrs. Pleasance and if *she* didn't know, *you* wouldn't know.

**LINGHAM** *moves to the stool and sits on it, facing* **ELSIE**.

And, of course, she asked a lot of awkward questions but I told her I don't know nothing, which is absolutely true.

**HENRIETTA** *rises and comes down to the foot of the stairs.*

I had a card, that's all. Sounded ever so cheerful but he didn't mention the job.

**FRANCES** *crosses and puts the laundry in the hall.*

Do you know if he'll still be wanting it? He's a marvellous bookkeeper.

**HENRIETTA** *(crossing to the chest down centre)* He *was* a lawyer. *(She sits on the floor above the left end of the chest.)*

**FRANCES** *(moving to right of the table)* Solicitor, Ettie.

**ELSIE** Yes, I know, dear, that's why he's such a marvellous bookkeeper, and I don't mind about the... *(She breaks off, realising that she is on a dangerous subject.)*

**FRANCES, HENRIETTA** *and* **LINGHAM** *react.*

Well, the man I have now is more reliable, of course, but he's got no personality. I can't stand him, but of course, I've got to let him know. *(She turns to* **FRANCES**.*)* Richard *is* better?

**FRANCES** *(pouring the tea)* Oh, yes, it's just that I don't know his plans.

**ELSIE** When exactly is he coming?

**FRANCES** Well, we don't quite...

**HENRIETTA** *Monday* or Tuesday.

**ELSIE** I do hope he wants it. The place has been like a morgue all day long without a laugh.

**HENRIETTA** *(icily)* I thought it was because of his bookkeeping.

**ELSIE** Well, partly, of course. Can't run a business on laughs.

LINGHAM *rises, crosses to the table, picks up a cup of tea and offers it to* ELSIE.

'Course, it caused a bit of trouble sometimes. *(She rises, moves to the bench left of the table and sits, facing* FRANCES.*)* I remember one lunch-time one of my regulars came to the shop at five to two. Well, officially, I don't open till two, but the poor old duck, she's a bit sour at the best of times – well, she peeped through the window, and Richard and me were having a game of draughts and she made a face – *(she demonstrates)* saying, "Let me in." D'you know what Richard did – he looked right back and blew some bubbles with his beer. *(She rises and moves to right of* LINGHAM.*)*

LINGHAM *again offers the cup of tea to* ELSIE.

*(Absorbed in her story, she ignores* LINGHAM *and sits on the downstage arm of the sofa.)* She just stood there, with her face getting longer than a ruler, and just as hard, and Richard kept blowing these bubbles – crawling up and down the counter, waggling his ears, with this old dear purple as a plum – and at the stroke of two – *(she rises and mimes the following as she speaks.)* he gets down off the counter, straightens his coat – ever so respectable, like a tailor's dummy – opens the door and bows. Well, she just started off down the street to tell her friends how she was never coming back to that madhouse... *(She breaks off, embarrassed at the implication she has made.)*

HENRIETTA *rises, moves to the armchair left chair, picks up the dress, then sits in the armchair.* FRANCES, *looking uncomfortable, continues to pour the tea.*

*(She sits on the downstage arm of the sofa. Lamely)* 'Course, I s'pose I should've opened the door – but that laugh was worth losing a customer any day. *(She rises and stands above the table.)* This geyser I've got still calls me "Miss Sharp", and the way he says it, really, it makes you grate your teeth. *(She suddenly sees* HENRIETTA*'s new dress.)* What a smashing dress!

FRANCES *sits on the bench right of the table.*

**HENRIETTA** *(rising)* I was just putting it away.

**ELSIE** *(crossing to right of* **HENRIETTA***)* Where are you going?

**HENRIETTA** I'm not going anywhere.

**ELSIE** *(coyly)* Well, you must be wearing it for something.

**LINGHAM** *(crossing below the sofa)* A birthday. *(He moves to the fireplace.)*

**ELSIE** *(to* **HENRIETTA***)* Your birthday? When is that?

**HENRIETTA** Next Wednesday.

**ELSIE** *(triumphantly)* I've got it!

**HENRIETTA** Got what?

**ELSIE** Why you're all looking so poker-faced. It's a surprise – and I know for who. *(She sits on the stool.)*

**HENRIETTA** What do you mean?

**ELSIE** Don't try and hide it. It's all over your faces.

> **LINGHAM** *moves to right of* **ELSIE** *and tries to cover up the horrifying mistake that he knows is about to be made.*

**LINGHAM** Oh, no, it's...

**ELSIE** *(interrupting)* I know what it is. It's a party. A surprise for Richard. What a lovely idea. *(She rises and moves to right of* **HENRIETTA***.)* He couldn't pick a nicer time to come home and the dress is really smashing. I think it needs a rose. Pop into the shop, dear, I do accessories, now. And long gloves, of course. *(archly)* Is there a boy friend coming?

**HENRIETTA** No.

**ELSIE** Bet there's someone you've got in mind.

> **HENRIETTA** *turns away and moves to the fireplace.*

'Course it's none of my business. Still, I do think it's a marvellous idea – all of it happening together. *(She turns to* **LINGHAM***.)* Don't you think so, Mr. Lingham? You know

Richard, how he really loves a get-together. *(She crosses and stands above the table.)* A party, eh, on Wednesday?

**LINGHAM** *(putting the cup of tea on the stool.)* I must clear up these things.

**ELSIE** And I must be going.

> **LINGHAM** *crosses to the hall, gets* **ELSIE**'s *wrap, puts it around her shoulders and opens the front door.*

Now, don't forget to pop across to the shop, dear. I've got ever such a nice choice of roses. A little present from me. *(to* **FRANCES***)* Now, don't get up. I'll let myself out. *(She moves to the hall.)* Well, back to old Hatchet-face. I will be glad to see Richard and I do hope he's coming back to me and I do think the party's a marvellous idea. I could read it all over your faces.

> **ELSIE** *exits by the front door.* **LINGHAM** *closes the door. There is a terrible silence, then* **LINGHAM** *crosses towards the door left.*

**LINGHAM** Please excuse me. *(He sees the cup of tea on the stool, stops, picks up the cup and puts it on the table.)*

**FRANCES** No tea, Mr. Lingham.

**LINGHAM** No, thank you. I have one or two things to do.

> **LINGHAM** *crosses and exits left, closing the door behind him.* **FRANCES** *rises and puts the cup on the tray.*

**HENRIETTA** *(moving centre)* Why didn't you tell her?

> **FRANCES** *picks up the tray and moves to the hall.*

*(she crosses to left of* **FRANCES***.th)* Why didn't you tell her Father won't be at the party?

**FRANCES** *(after a pause; turning to face* **HENRIETTA***)* I was too ashamed.

> **FRANCES** *exits to the kitchen.* **HENRIETTA** *shrugs her shoulders as – the curtain falls.*

## Scene Two

*Scene – the same. Later the same evening.*

*When the curtain rises, the stool and the armchair left centre have been moved nearer to the up left corner of the chest down centre.* LINGHAM *is seated in the armchair left centre.* HENRIETTA *is seated on the up left corner of the chest down centre. The stool is between them and they are playing draughts. After a moment,* HENRIETTA *rises, moves to the footstool above the armchair left centre and sits.*

LINGHAM  Another game, Ettie?

HENRIETTA  All right, but you always win.

LINGHAM  Well, I did practise all last winter. That's what comes of doing the same thing over and over. I dig myself a nice little hole and get fond of the things around me. *(He leans back in his chair.)*

*HENRIETTA rises, moves behind* LINGHAM's *chair and leans on the back of it.*

I can get fond of things simply because I look at them for a long time. Simply because they're there.

HENRIETTA  But you have to like something because it's *something*. *(She moves left of* LINGHAM.*)*

LINGHAM  If I took that view no-one would like me. That's why I never moved from my job. Now, you take Miss Willings – she's the secretary. Do you know, I think she's quite fond of me.

HENRIETTA  *(crossing above* LINGHAM *to right of him)* That's because you're so – well, so...

LINGHAM  Just *there*, Ettie. *(He sets out the draughtsmen.)* Your move first.

HENRIETTA  *(moving down centre and looking at* LINGHAM*)* Haven't you ever wanted to stride through the world, picking up this and throwing away that?

**LINGHAM** I'd be too frightened that some other strider might throw me away.

**HENRIETTA** Well, that's the point. One mustn't *be* frightened.

**LINGHAM** You've only just left school, Ettie.

**HENRIETTA** I'll never be frightened. But it's different for you. You haven't got anyone to live up to. *(She kneels beside* **LINGHAM.***)* Oh, I'm sorry, I didn't mean it like that.

**LINGHAM** You're quite right, of course. Perhaps that's why I never married. I was afraid of being pushed. Do you know what would happen to me if I were pushed, Ettie?

**HENRIETTA** Tell me.

**LINGHAM** *(half-smiling)* I'd just fall over.

**HENRIETTA** *(rising and moving to the fireplace)* No – you'd be the president of the biggest bank in the world.

**LINGHAM** Who would I be fond of?

**HENRIETTA** Your wife. Someone beautiful and haughty, like Mother.

**LINGHAM** But your mother's not haughty.

**HENRIETTA** No, but she would be if she were married to you, the president of the biggest bank in the world and she'd live in a candle-lit castle.

**LINGHAM** What would she do while this banker was banking?

**HENRIETTA** *(moving down centre; giving herself away without thinking)* Look after her children.

**LINGHAM** I can't quite fit your mother into that picture.

**HENRIETTA** *(carrying fantasy into realism)* That's because no-one treats her like a queen. She can't *like* being a wet-nurse, can she? She can't *like* doing this horrible job in the evenings? Having a husband who works in the nylon shop across the road – who's kept on because he's a sort of a clown.

LINGHAM  Oh, I don't think Miss Sharp meant it like that.

HENRIETTA  She said he was funny.

LINGHAM  Humorous – that's what she meant.

HENRIETTA  *Funny.* Everyone thinks he's funny. I think he begs
with his jokes. Oh, I hate his jokes.

LINGHAM  Ettie, I don't think we should speak of it.

HENRIETTA  *(insisting) Begs* with his jokes, and Mother feeds him
pity – *(she moves to the fireplace)* and you play draughts and
buy him books about birds.

LINGHAM  Please, Ettie, let's play another game.

HENRIETTA  You know, I wish he'd never come back.

LINGHAM  *(horrified)* Ettie!

HENRIETTA  I don't care what you think. I wish he'd never come
back. *(She turns and leans on her hands on the mantelpiece.)*

*The front door bell rings.* LINGHAM *rises, crosses and
opens the front door.*

ELSIE *enters by the front door. She carries a small box of
artificial roses.*

SOYA MARSHALL *follows her on. He is aged about nineteen
and has a simple, shy manner. He is wearing a suede
jacket and carrying a crash helmet.*

ELSIE  *(as she enters)* Hello, Mr. Lingham. I'm back again.

SOYA *crosses below* LINGHAM *to right of* ELSIE.

You can't get rid of me, can you?

LINGHAM *closes the door.*

HENRIETTA  *(bewildered at seeing* ELSIE *and* SOYA *together)* Yes?
*(She moves to left, of the sofa.)*

ELSIE *(pleased because of the situation; coyly)* Well, I know why I'm here but I don't know about this young man. We walked up together and before I knew it we were pushing the same bell. I mean, we both scrambled for it. He won. *(She looks* SOYA *up and down.)* But then, of course, he's bigger than me. *(She smiles at* SOYA.*)* I saw you ride up on your scooter but I never dreamt that you were coming here.

SOYA I'm Soya Marshall.

ELSIE *(embarrassed)* Oh, I'm sorry. I thought you two knew each other. Naturally – ah – well, I would, wouldn't I?

HENRIETTA *(furious because* ELSIE *and* SOYA *have arrived together)* Well, come in. *(She sits on the sofa.)*

SOYA *stands above the table.* ELSIE *crosses to the stool, taking a garish, artificial red rose from the box as she does so.* LINGHAM *crosses quickly in front of* ELSIE, *takes the draughts board and men from the stool and puts them on the chest.*

ELSIE I popped across because I brought the roses. *(She holds up the rose.)* There, how about that? *(She puts the box on the stool.)*

LINGHAM *moves to the bookshelves left.*

"Blush red", that one's called.

HENRIETTA *does not react.*

Oh, well. *(She turns to* LINGHAM.*)* How about that, Mr. Lingham?

LINGHAM Very nice. Blush red, eh?

ELSIE Don't you think it's got something?

LINGHAM Oh, yes, indeed.

HENRIETTA *(to* SOYA; *quietly)* Hello.

ELSIE *(looking at* SOYA *and* HENRIETTA) Oh, I *am* sorry. *(She turns, takes some more roses from the box and spreads them on the stool.)* I do keep forgetting that you two don't know each other.

HENRIETTA *(introducing)* Soya Marshall – Mr. Lingham. He's a friend – *(she is determined to avoid the word "lodger")* and Miss Sharp. *(She is also determined to make it clear that her relationship with* ELSIE *is entirely business.)*

LINGHAM *moves up left.*

ELSIE *(turning to look at* HENRIETTA *and* SOYA*)* Doesn't it sound terrible – "Miss Sharp"? I thought once of changing it.

HENRIETTA *(coldly)* Miss Sharp is here because I am *buying* some roses from her.

ELSIE *(not realising that she is being snubbed)* Not real ones, of course. I keep a ladies' shop. *(She moves up centre.)* I do a bit of gents' stuff as well. As a matter of fact, Ettie's father...

LINGHAM *(moving left; hastily interrupting)* The roses are lovely.

ELSIE *(with a step towards* LINGHAM; *pleased)* Do you think so? I think it will really set the dress off. *(She holds the rose next to herself and turns to* SOYA.*)* Shoulder or here? What do you think? Let's have a young man's opinion.

SOYA *(moving right of the downstage end of the sofa; shyly, but he likes* ELSIE*)* Either way seems very nice to me.

ELSIE Oh, come on, you can do better than that. Let's try it on the birthday girl. *(She holds the rose against* HENRIETTA*'s right shoulder.)*

SOYA *(leaning over the back of the sofa; genuinely)* It's lovely.

LINGHAM Quite lovely.

ELSIE On white, of course. Well, you'll see it. You'll be coming on the birthday. On white, you'll really get the full effect. *(She turns to* SOYA.*)* You are coming to the birthday?

LINGHAM *moves above the armchair left centre.*

SOYA Well, that's what I called about.

**HENRIETTA** You can come?

**ELSIE** Oh, you mustn't miss it. It'll really be a do, I can promise you.

**LINGHAM** *(desperately realising that dates are about to come out)* I wonder if you'd care for a game of draughts, Miss Sharp?

**ELSIE** *(surprised but pleased)* Draughts? *(She drops the rose in* **HENRIETTA***'s lap.)* What a marvellous idea. *(She crosses to* **LINGHAM***.)* I haven't had a game since...

**ELSIE** *is about to mention* **RICHARD** *again, but* **LINGHAM** *swiftly interrupts.*

**LINGHAM** *(collecting the draughts from the chest)* In my room, if that's all right. *(He crosses to the door left)* There is a table and two very comfortable armchairs.

**ELSIE** *(following* **LINGHAM***)* Well, that is nice. *(She stops, turns and moves centre.)* No, I've got a much better idea. Come across to my place. I've got a flagon... You do *like* beer?

**LINGHAM** Yes, most certainly.

**ELSIE** I could make a little bite. Oh, dear, I hope the beer's not flat. *(She has the natural anxiety of one who has never been loved.)* And cold ham. You do *like* ham?

**LINGHAM** It's most kind of you.

**ELSIE** Not at all. I'd love a bit of company. I really hate being on my own.

**LINGHAM** *(looking towards* **HENRIETTA** *and* **SOYA***)* Would you two excuse us?

**HENRIETTA** *(rising and looking at* **LINGHAM** *with enormous gratitude)* Yes, of course.

**ELSIE** Well, bring the board, Mr. Lingham. *(She moves to the stool, puts the roses in the box and picks it up.)*

**LINGHAM** *goes to the bookshelves left and puts the draughts in their box.*

HENRIETTA  How much do I owe you for the rose?

ELSIE  It's a present, dear. I don't want anything for it. I'm just glad you're pleased. *(She crosses to* SOYA.*)* Well, ever so glad to have met you. Wasn't it funny bumping into you like that. Do you live around here?

SOYA  No, Miss Sharp.

ELSIE  "Miss Sharp" – doesn't it sound terrible? Do you know, Ettie's father is the only one I know who can say that name without making me feel like vinegar. Of course, he has a real way with him.

LINGHAM  *(crossing with the box and board to* ELSIE*)* Coming, Miss Sharp.

ELSIE  Oh, let me carry the board. *(She takes the draught board from* LINGHAM.*)*

LINGHAM *goes to the front door and opens it.*

A game of draughts – how nice. *(She moves to* LINGHAM *then turns to the others.)* Well, toodle-oo. *(She turns to* LINGHAM. *Anxiously)* You're sure you like ham?

LINGHAM  Oh, quite. *(to* SOYA*)* Well, good night.

SOYA  Goodnight, sir. Enjoy the game.

ELSIE  Well, I will, I'm sure. *(she winks)* Enjoy yourselves, too.

ELSIE *and* LINGHAM *exit by the front door, closing it after them.*

SOYA  *(looking after* ELSIE*)* She seems very fond of draughts. *(He turns to* HENRIETTA.*)*

HENRIETTA  *(sitting on the sofa; holding the rose)* Yes, she is. Silly, isn't it?

*From this moment onwards,* HENRIETTA *is caught in a web of lies. Her determination to create a picture of her background which she feels will impress* SOYA *makes her whole manner tense and, at moments when the truth seems near, she is bordering on hysteria.* SOYA, *naïve and direct, is continually confused by her strange behaviour but he is always attracted to her.*

SOYA Where will you wear the rose?

HENRIETTA *(putting the rose on the downstage arm of the sofa)* Oh, I don't really want to wear it at all.

SOYA I think she'd be upset.

HENRIETTA Oh, she won't be here.

SOYA *(surprised)* Oh, I didn't know. From the way she spoke I thought...

HENRIETTA *(looking away)* She bothers Father all the time.

SOYA *moves below the sofa, puts his helmet on the downstage end of the sofa, picks up the rose and moves to left of* HENRIETTA.

He helped her once with her books – in a friendly way. Someone told him she was in a muddle. Ever since then she keeps bothering him and he's too nice to tell her.

SOYA What do I call you?

HENRIETTA "Ettie", of course. Nobody calls me "Henrietta", except Father. It suits him to say Henrietta. He's sort of strict and aloof.

SOYA Sounds frightening.

HENRIETTA He is, a little. He lives in such an important world, all of his own. You are coming to the party?

SOYA I'm really nervous of meeting your father.

HENRIETTA He won't be there. He's away and I couldn't ask him to come home just for a party. He wouldn't enjoy being with a lot of kids. You *will* come?

SOYA *(referring to* LINGHAM*)* The old man seems nice. I think he only went to please her – or us.

**HENRIETTA** Oh, he's sweet. He's a friend, he's staying here. Father's a little sorry for him, so concerned with little things.

**SOYA** Your father?

**HENRIETTA** No – Mr. Lingham. You know, birds and draughts.

**SOYA** How do you mean – birds?

**HENRIETTA** He cuts them out and pastes them in a book.

**SOYA** I used to do that. Not birds, but engines.

> **HENRIETTA** *turns slowly and looks at* **SOYA***, puzzled.* **SOYA** *turns away left, realising he has made a "faux pas".*

No reason, I just used to cut them out.

**HENRIETTA** *(rising)* But he's fifty-seven.

**SOYA** He looks more than that – well, it just got to be a habit, I expect. Where does he find them?

**HENRIETTA** What?

**SOYA** These birds.

**HENRIETTA** *(exasperated)* Anywhere. Magazines. Anywhere.

**SOYA** *(turning to face her)* Same with me and the engines.

**HENRIETTA** *(moving below the sofa; condescendingly)* I hope you didn't mind me asking you to the party. Of course, you're not obliged to come.

**SOYA** I know, but when Paula Wright told me your name, it meant something. Henrietta Brough – I knew that name.

**HENRIETTA** I was at Alison Verney's party last summer. That's where I saw you.

**SOYA** No, it's further back than that. Connected with something – some incident.

**HENRIETTA** I don't know what you mean.

**SOYA** Yes, some incident. And when I saw you at the door I remembered your face. That same funny look, as though someone had caught you with your hair down. Perhaps you didn't like me just turning up like that, but that's me, I'm afraid. I just hop on my scooter and turn up.

HENRIETTA *(moving centre; sharply)* Don't ever do that to me. Don't ever turn up.

SOYA But you look lovely with your hair down, Ettie.

HENRIETTA Do I?

SOYA *(moving to left of* HENRIETTA*)* You should wear the rose in your hair. *(He holds the rose against* HENRIETTA*'s hair.)*

HENRIETTA *moves quickly to the chest down centre and lies on it.*

HENRIETTA I haven't quite decided how to decorate the room.

SOYA *moves down left.*

I thought Chinese lanterns. They make sweet soft little lights and I'm going to move all those books from the shelves and put candles, like a Christmas tree. You *are* coming? I love the evening because of the little lights. It makes everything so precious and you have to tip-toe so you won't disturb anything.

SOYA *(looking at the books on the shelves left)* Who studies law?

HENRIETTA Father's a lawyer, but he's retired now.

SOYA *(turning to her)* Oh, I imagined him young.

HENRIETTA He is, but – but – *(she cannot think of a lie)* but practising bored him, so now he stays home and does – hm – research.

SOYA Is he writing a book?

HENRIETTA Yes, something like that. *(She giggles self-consciously.)* It's all so clever I hardly know what it is.

SOYA *(moving slowly to left of* HENRIETTA*)* There, you have that funny look on your face again.

HENRIETTA *(sitting up on the right side of the chest)* What funny look?

SOYA As though you were going to cry.

HENRIETTA What a silly idea. I hardly ever cry.

SOYA *(moving above the chest)* Are you disappointed that your father can't come to the party?

HENRIETTA Of course not. He – he's much too busy – I wouldn't expect him to.

SOYA *(worried by her manner)* Are you sure there's nothing wrong?

HENRIETTA *(lying on the chest)* Nothing, absolutely nothing. Except – I just can't decide about the candles.

SOYA *moves up centre.*

Pink is more precious but green is eerie.

SOYA *(turning to* HENRIETTA*)* I hope my scooter is all right.

HENRIETTA It must be wonderful to ride a scooter. Riding with the world, completely in control.

SOYA *(moving above the chest; naïvely)* I saw a boy go under a bus yesterday. He didn't look where he was going.

HENRIETTA Oh, you'll always look where you are going. The first time I saw you, you had on that suede jacket. I said, "There's someone who'll stride through the world."

*This is the first time that* HENRIETTA *has touched on an important aspect of* SOYA*'s personality.*

SOYA If I can just get through my exams.

HENRIETTA *sits up on the right end of the chest.*

Trouble is, they scare me. It's like being put on trial.

HENRIETTA Oh, you mustn't be frightened.

SOYA *(squatting on the floor left of the chest, facing* HENRIETTA*)* I can't think where I saw you. Did you always live here?

HENRIETTA *(leaning down and facing* SOYA*)* No, we had a little house with turrets, over the hill. My room had a window like a church. Down below were marigolds like a great orange cloak. You could see them if you leaned far out of my window. The house was sold when Father retired... *(She breaks off hectically.)* Of course, it's of no importance. *(She looks front.)* A house is such a messy thing. You never know where you'll find yourself next.

SOYA Have I upset you by just calling?

HENRIETTA Upset me – I was just waiting – I mean I was just waiting for Mother.

SOYA Will she be back soon?

HENRIETTA She takes evening classes. How to make little – *(she stops, but too late, she has said it)* mats.

SOYA Mats?

HENRIETTA And if they make the mats well, they cover tops of chairs in raffia. *(she laughs)*

SOYA She likes it?

HENRIETTA Of course, otherwise, why would she do it? Father thinks it's very funny.

SOYA *(simply)* Why?

HENRIETTA *(turning slowly to* SOYA; *surprised)* Well, don't you?

SOYA No, but I suppose it must be to him.

HENRIETTA Why should you think that? You've never met him.

SOYA No, but I feel as though I have. I never met anyone who talked so much about their father.

HENRIETTA Do I talk a lot about him.

SOYA All the time.

HENRIETTA *(rising)* I'm sorry. *(She moves and leans on the armchair above the table.)*

SOYA Oh, it doesn't matter. *(He puts the role on the chest, rises and moves centre.)* I wish I had someone to talk of me like that.

HENRIETTA I bet your mother and father are really mad about you.

SOYA Well, not exactly. *(He moves below the sofa.)* Of course, if I can just get through these exams.

HENRIETTA *(sitting on the upstage end of the table and facing* SOYA*)* But you will, of course. It's just a matter of confidence.

SOYA Well, I sit home most nights with the books, but – nothing. Figures just laugh at me. I keep staring at them but they never get together to make any sense and then I get this sick feeling and my head feels terrible. *(He sits on the sofa.)* Then mum or dad comes in with tea and says, "How's it going?"

HENRIETTA And what do you say?

SOYA "Fine, thanks." When I really feel bad, I cut out the engines. I hate exams. It's as though I'm on trial.

HENRIETTA What do you like?

SOYA Cars.

HENRIETTA What do you mean?

SOYA Just messing with them.

HENRIETTA *rises and crosses to left of* SOYA.

HENRIETTA *(after a pause; open-eyed)* Forever?

SOYA *(looking up at her)* That's right.

HENRIETTA *(facing front)* Perhaps one day, you'll be head of a big industry.

SOYA No. As Dad says, without the figures, where are you?

HENRIETTA *turns to* SOYA.

Just messing about in overalls and it's overalls that really gets him and he draws the line between jeans and overalls.

HENRIETTA He does? How?

SOYA If they've got a bib front, that's overalls. I went into the lounge once. I didn't know he was home. He was entertaining some business associates. When he saw the overalls, he went purple and then he started to tell these men about me and the figures.

**HENRIETTA** About how you can't do them? How terrible!

**SOYA** No, worse than that. How I'm a mathematical genius. Now, I avoid both men in the street, I'm always afraid they might ask me to add up something. Yet, messing about with cars, I feel like a king. Trouble is, I don't look like one.

**HENRIETTA** *smiles and moves to the fireplace.*

*(he leans back)* How do you feel about someone lying under a car, Ettie?

**HENRIETTA** *(refusing to look the facts in the face)* Oh, that's not important. Because I'm absolutely sure that you'll own fleets of cars, grey and sleek and they won't have any drivers. They'll go all by themselves.

**SOYA** There, you've got that look again. Where did I see you, Ettie? It was somewhere with a crowd of people.

**HENRIETTA** *(lost in fantasy)* And you'll sit up in a huge tower, watching your beautiful cars glide by.

**SOYA** Wish I could remember where I've seen you.

**HENRIETTA** *(crossing to the armchair left centre)* You are *coming* to the party? *(She curls up in the armchair.)*

**SOYA** Well, that's what I've been trying to tell you. My exam is Saturday. I'm taking it at Manchester.

**HENRIETTA** *(relieved)* Well, that's fine – 'cause the party's Sunday.

**SOYA** Yes – but I've got to stay the night with my Uncle Willie. He lives just outside the town.

**HENRIETTA** Why?

**SOYA** Well – my mother's got a sort of thing about Uncle Willie. He's the bright star in our family. That's how I got my name. *(He rises)*

**HENRIETTA** Soya?

**SOYA** *nods.*

It's a wonderful name.

**SOYA** *(moving centre)* I hate it. Uncle Willie wrote a book about someone who climbed mountains all the time. I *read* it. I didn't get it. Anyway, Mother named me after the mountain climber.

**HENRIETTA** So your uncle's a writer?

**SOYA** No – he never wrote anything else. He owns a chain of butcher shops. Anyway, I've got to spend Sunday with him. If I could catch the five o'clock train, I could be here at nine-thirty.

**HENRIETTA** Well, that's fine. After all, parties just go on and on.

**SOYA** Would it really be all right to come late? I might even be able to get away but I couldn't promise.

**HENRIETTA** Well, try – but if you can't, then come by half past nine. You will come?

**SOYA** I won't be much fun after all those figures.

**HENRIETTA** *(looking front)* You'll see. They'll fall into place, quite suddenly.

**SOYA** But if they don't. Would you mind about the overalls?

**HENRIETTA** But they *will.*

**SOYA** *(moving up centre)* But if they don't, Ettie, would you mind?

**HENRIETTA** They *will.*

**FRANCES** *enters by the front door. She carries her bucket bag.*

**FRANCES** *(coming into the room)* Oh, I am so tired, Ettie. Those rooms are so draughty... *(She sees* **SOYA***.)* Oh, hello.

**HENRIETTA** *(rising and crossing to left of the sofa)* Mother, this is Soya Marshall – this is my mother.

**SOYA** *(crossing below* **HENRIETTA** *to left of* **FRANCES***)* How do you do, Mrs. Brough? *(He shakes hands with* **FRANCES***.)*

FRANCES How do you do?

SOYA *(embarrassed)* Well, I must be going. *(He collects his crash helmet.)*

FRANCES *(turning and putting her bucket bag and handbag on the table)* Oh, must you?

SOYA I'm afraid so. I've got some work to do. I'll see you at the party.

FRANCES *(turning to SOYA)* I'm glad you're coming.

SOYA So am I. *(He moves to the hall.)* See you Sunday, Ettie.

FRANCES *moves below the sofa and removes her raincoat.*

*(he frowns, stops suddenly and turns)* Excuse me, but I remember now where I saw both of you before. I've been trying to remember all the evening and seeing you together it's just come back to me. It was a Parents' Day at Ilford Park School. You must have gone there, Ettie, to Ilford Park. I remember you leaving early. It was Parents' Day. Everyone stood aside and you walked down the aisle. *(He recalls this slowly in his mind.)* Wasn't somebody taken ill or something? That's right. It's a few years ago but I remember you both. You were helping some man.

FRANCES It was Ettie's father. He was taken ill. *(She takes HENRIETTA's hand and grips it.)*

HENRIETTA *(swiftly)* A heart attack.

SOYA Oh, I hope he's well now.

HENRIETTA Oh, yes, he's fine. We'll see you Sunday.

SOYA Good-bye, Mrs. Brough.

FRANCES Good-bye.

HENRIETTA Good luck.

SOYA Thanks, and I'll be as quick as I can.

SOYA *exits by the front door.* HENRIETTA *moves to the armchair left centre.* FRANCES *puts her raincoat on the sofa and turns to* HENRIETTA.

FRANCES *(removing her gloves)* Seems a nice boy.

HENRIETTA Oh, he's wonderful, isn't he?

FRANCES Seems a really good boy.

HENRIETTA Oh, he's much more than that.

FRANCES *(with a step or two towards* HENRIETTA*)* He has a good memory. He remembers you from Ilford Park.

HENRIETTA Oh, he'll forget about it.

FRANCES What did you say about your father?

HENRIETTA *(sitting in the armchair left centre; casually)* It didn't come up.

FRANCES *(moving centre; ruthlessly)* It came up just a moment ago.

HENRIETTA *(turning on* FRANCES *with growing anger; with slow precision)* Well, what could I have said? Yes, I remember Ilford Park School and I remember that particular Parents' Day and the aisle and I remember the people standing aside and everyone watching and I remember holding father's arm tight – tight, like it would break, like I was willing him to stand on his feet – and I remember the silence in those searching eyes and how he suddenly tripped and I grabbed him for fear he'd fall at my feet, my own father, a drunken bundle of something...

FRANCES Don't say that. He's not a drunk. But you know why it happened, Ettie. Because you didn't want him there. Because you didn't want him at the Parents' Day.

HENRIETTA How can I want him?

FRANCES Try, Ettie, try and want him.

HENRIETTA I can't.

FRANCES You've got to, Ettie – this is *his home.*

**HENRIETTA** And *mine* – but you don't care about me at all – do you? Only about him – I know that.

**FRANCES** It's not true – I'm thinking of you, too – this boy – such a nice boy, Ettie, sometime he'll want to meet your father.

**HENRIETTA** (*rising and moving to left of* FRANCES; *stonily*) Not Sunday.

**FRANCES** (*pleading*) Please, Ettie, listen to me – he's much better.

**HENRIETTA** *Not* Sunday – supposing something happened.

**FRANCES** Nothing will happen – if you have some faith – just don't watch him – just don't wait for something to happen – try and *look* as though you love him a little.

**HENRIETTA** (*turning away above the armchair left centre; bitterly*) Him – him – you only care about him – but he's not going to spoil my party. I want it to be beautiful, and he's not going to spoil it – you can stop him coming.

**FRANCES** (*moving away right centre*) I can't do it – don't ask me.

**HENRIETTA** (*moving to left of* FRANCES) If you stop him coming – I'll be nice to him after Sunday. I'll do anything *after* Sunday. (*She turns away and throws herself into the armchair left centre.*) You don't want to spoil my party – do you?

**FRANCES** (*weakening*) No – I don't want to spoil it – but what can I say to him? In the letter this morning he says he's much better. – He's *got to come back*, Ettie.

**HENRIETTA** Monday.

**FRANCES** (*frantically*) This is his *home.*

**HENRIETTA** Monday. If he made a mess of my party, I'd never forgive you.

**FRANCES** (*after a pause; beaten*) All right. (*She crosses to the telephone, lifts the receiver and dials T-O-L. Into the telephone*) Get me Pincer seven-six-four-five. This is Kilburn double-eight-two-one.

HENRIETTA *(crying)* He'll believe you. *(She reaches out and touches* FRANCES*'s arm.)* You can say anything and he'll believe you.

FRANCES *pushes* HENRIETTA*'s hand away and speaks with no affection in her voice.* HENRIETTA *is just an enemy.*

FRANCES  Be quiet, Ettie!

HENRIETTA  You do understand, don't you? Say you understand.

FRANCES  *(tonelessly)* Yes, I understand. *(into the telephone)* Is Dr Cawley there? ...It's Frances Brough...

HENRIETTA  *(her fists clenched tightly)* What will you say?

FRANCES  Be quiet, Ettie.

HENRIETTA *buries her face in her hands.*

*(into the telephone)* Dr Cawley? ...It's Frances Brough... How are you? ...It's about my husband... Well, you know Richard would like to come home this weekend and there's a personal matter that makes it very difficult... I wonder if you could use your influence and keep him there till Monday, without mentioning that I've phoned, of course... Well, naturally I would love to see Richard, but circumstances have arisen which are completely beyond my control... Thank you, Doctor. *(She slowly replaces the receiver and crosses above the armchair to right of it.)*

HENRIETTA  *(groping for* FRANCES *with her right hand)* Say you understand. Say you understand.

FRANCES *turns, smiles and takes* HENRIETTA *in her arms as – the curtain falls.*

## Scene Three

*Scene – the same. Two days later. 5.30 p.m.*

*When the curtain rises, the lights are on. A string of Chinese lanterns has been hung over the fireplace, there are small decorative candles on the bookshelves left and there is a lantern on the chest down centre. The lanterns and candles are lit. The armchair left centre is back in its original position and the stool is in front of the fireplace, opened out to form steps.* FRANCES *is on the stool-steps adjusting the lanterns over the fireplace.* LINGHAM *is standing left of the sofa, holding another, unlit, lantern.*

FRANCES How does that look?

LINGHAM *steps back and looks up at the lantern.*

LINGHAM A little crooked – tip it slightly over to the left.

FRANCES *adjusts a lantern.*

Ah, perfect. It really looks most effective.

FRANCES Do you think that's enough?

LINGHAM Yes, I think so. *(He moves to the steps.)* Discretion is very important in decorations.

LINGHAM *helps* FRANCES *down from the steps.*

FRANCES *(smiling)* You think discretion is *important.* I don't think I've ever really heard you come out with anything.

LINGHAM Well, being a lodger closes one up a little. One has to be careful about one's rights. It has taught me not to expect anything. *(He hands the lantern to* FRANCES.*)*

FRANCES *closes the lantern and moves to the armchair left centre.*

Henrietta thinks that's wrong.

FRANCES *looks away.*

*(He looks at the lanterns.)* That lantern's not quite straight, you know. *(He goes up the steps and straightens a lantern.)*

FRANCES Oh, bother the thing.

LINGHAM Well, one must have order somewhere. *(He comes down from the steps.)* Right thing?

FRANCES Oh, don't look at me as if you're not understanding. I love him.

LINGHAM Yes, I know.

FRANCES The first time I saw him – at a students' dance, there was a whole group of people around him. He was talking and laughing, and everyone was listening so attentively. Then someone made a cutting remark. I can't even remember what it was. Trivial – but piercing. I saw the needle go home and his eyes started to blink and everything left him – all the vitality. The people began to drift away and he was alone.

LINGHAM *(moving to the bench left of the table)* And then he started to drink.

FRANCES To hide that loneliness, Harold. *(She rises and moves centre.)* Somehow he has to hide that loneliness. *(with a nervous laugh)* I thought I could do it, Harold – I thought I could creep into those dark places.

LINGHAM And you have.

FRANCES Yes, but he doesn't know I'm there... *(she breaks off)* Ettie thinks I was tricked. *(She moves to the chest down centre.)*

LINGHAM Why are you telling me this? *(He sits on the bench left of the table.)*

FRANCES Because of tonight. *(She sits on the right end of the chest, facing LINGHAM.)* Have I done a terrible thing? Everything went well the first years of our marriage. Sometimes little things happened and I coped with them. Richard seemed happy. I got rid of anyone who might cut at his confidence. He had difficult moments in his work, but his home was a place where I could nurse him. Then an enemy arrived, someone I couldn't get rid of. Henrietta was born. She found him out early. She would stare at him as a child. Tiny child, staring at him, daring his eyes to blink. He'd stop in the middle of sentences and correct himself. Once, when he was telling her a story, she said, "What's a hero, Father?" and Richard said, "A hero's a man who's not afraid" – *(She is beginning to break down.)* and she looked at him with such a merciless gaze that I was reminded of the first time I'd seen him with the people walking away – so alone.

**LINGHAM**  But you've had faith.

**FRANCES**  But he doesn't need it from me. He needs it from Henrietta. *(She rises and puts the lantern in the chest.)* Funny, I hardly ever call her "Henrietta" and I think Richard is afraid to say "Ettie". *(The tears run down her face.)*

**LINGHAM**  *(rising)* And they've never talked about it.

**FRANCES**  Never. Ettie just avoids him.

**LINGHAM**  *(crossing to the armchair left centre)* Sometimes when he comes to my room, we speak of Henrietta.

**FRANCES**  What does he say?

**LINGHAM**  *(moving below the armchair left centre)* "A wonderful girl, that. What a wonderful daughter."

**FRANCES**  And they never speak to each other. Hardly anything since that Parents' Day. Do you remember?

**LINGHAM**  Yes, I remember.

**FRANCES**  You didn't see everything. You left at the door of Henrietta's room. Ettie and I got him onto her bed. He was sick. She looked at him and she was completely rigid. "All over my beautiful cover", she said, and then she ran into my room. When I looked at Richard he was crying.

**LINGHAM**  Oh, Frances, I wish I could say something.

FRANCES *(pulling herself together)* I'm just glad you rent the room.

LINGHAM But why? If Ettie had her hero, I wouldn't be here. If only I could be got rid of in some way and that little room closed. Sometimes I think, Frances, if I could blot myself out, I could blot out your trouble with it.

FRANCES Oh, don't say that.

HENRIETTA *rushes in by the front door, breathless with excitement. She carries three packets of biscuits.* FRANCES *and* LINGHAM *move to the stool and fold the steps.*

HENRIETTA *(moving left of the table)* I've got them, and two more packets of crackers as well. I couldn't get the salty ones. *(She looks at the lanterns.)* Lovely. Don't they look sweet? *(She runs to the light switches at the foot of the stairs.)* Let's try them with the lights out. *(She switches out the lights and moves down right to see the effect.)* There, how wonderful. Everything looks a little unreal. *(She moves to the switches.)* Mustn't burn up the atmosphere. *(She switches on the lights and moves to left, of the table.)* I must save it. What time is it?

LINGHAM *(looking at his watch)* Twenty to six.

HENRIETTA It just rushes away. Everything simply pounds towards the party. Now, I've got the crackers. *(She puts the packets on the upstage end of the table.)* Is there anything else I've forgotten?

FRANCES Do you want the long gloves from Elsie?

HENRIETTA *(turning to FRANCES)* But how can I go there? She doesn't know the party's tonight. She waved from her window as I was coming in but I couldn't go across. I can't ask for the gloves. Would you go?

FRANCES Me?

HENRIETTA *(sitting on the bench left of the table)* Well, you can handle her and she embarrasses me. You could say that you wanted to try them next to the dress.

**FRANCES** All right. *(She goes to the hall.)*

**HENRIETTA** Thank you. That'll give me time to go across to Paula's before I dress.

**FRANCES** *exits by the front door.*

*(she rises)* Don't you think he's a wonderful boy, Mr. Lingham?

**LINGHAM** Who's that?

**HENRIETTA** Why, Soya Marshall. Don't you think he looks like really *somebody* – as though inside he all fits together? And when we met, it was so incredible. We understood each other perfectly.

**LINGHAM** That's a very rare thing. Perfect understanding.

**HENRIETTA** But you know when it's there. When someone understands your dreams. *(She moves to **LINGHAM**.)* Suddenly, your thoughts meet – *(She flings her arms around **LINGHAM**.)* and you're – *(She imitates her words and goes to the front door.)* flying away.

**LINGHAM** Where is he now?

**HENRIETTA** *(jerked out of her fantasy)* Who?

**LINGHAM** Mr. Marshall.

**HENRIETTA** Oh, *he's* in Manchester, sitting an exam.

**HENRIETTA** *runs out by the front door, slamming it behind her.*

**LINGHAM** *stands quietly for a moment, then picks up the packets of biscuits and exits to the kitchen. He re-enters, crosses to centre and stands brooding a moment, then stands on the stool and adjusts a lantern. The front door opens, but **LINGHAM** does not hear it.*

**RICHARD BROUGH** *enters by the front door. He is a large, powerfully built man. He carries a small suitcase. He creeps up behind **LINGHAM** and speaks in a boisterously teasing voice. All his movements are lion-sized.*

**RICHARD** Old Leaky-Jugs.

**LINGHAM** *(turning; startled)* Mr. Brough!

**RICHARD** *(roaring with laughter)* Mr. Brough. *(He puts his suitcase under the table.)* Leaky-Jugs, you're the most formal old bird that ever lived. Richard's my name, now try it.

**LINGHAM** *(getting down from the stool)* Richard, what are you doing here?

**RICHARD** *(raising his eyebrows)* What am I doing here? I've come home, Harold. *(He slaps* **LINGHAM** *on the back.)* I've come home to improve your game. All the way back in the train, I've been thinking, of all those in need of me, Harold's going to benefit most. No more pottering around, Harold. Concentrated effort. Don't look so desperate. I won't barrage you this evening. *(He looks around and points to the lantern on the chest down centre.)* The place looks wonderful. What's that?

**LINGHAM** A lantern.

**RICHARD** A lantern. Yes, I can see that, Harold, but what's it doing there? No, don't answer. To light up the room. You'll give away nothing, will you, Harold? When you die, I'll put on your epitaph "Old Leaky-Jugs, spiller of milk, but never of secrets." Well, you secret lantern, what will you light up tonight? *(He moves above the table, takes off his hat and flings it on the bench right of the table.)* Do you know, Harold, Dr Cawley tried to stop me coming today. "Go Monday," he said. "Go to one of your own padded cells," I said.

**LINGHAM** *(horrified)* Padded cells?

**RICHARD** *(enjoying teasing him)* I exaggerate, of course. Point of fact, they were rather bright little bed-sitters. I don't think it helped, though. Chintz, if anything, emphasizes the agony. If they flung you into an old sewer. I think one would feel better by comparison.

**LINGHAM** Was it very bad?

RICHARD *(moving to right of* LINGHAM *and putting an arm around his shoulders)* You'll make me think it was Purgatory if you don't take that racks and thumbscrews off your face. I thought by the time I came back you'd have lost that two-pound-twelve-and-sixpenny-lodger look. *(gently)* Don't you feel at all at home yet, Harold?

LINGHAM This is not my home, Richard.

RICHARD I say it is. *(He slaps* LINGHAM *on the back.)* You're a good sort, Harold. Now, where is my wife?

LINGHAM Frances?

RICHARD Well, she is still my wife, isn't she?

LINGHAM Of course.

RICHARD Where is she?

LINGHAM She's out.

RICHARD *(laughing at* LINGHAM*'s embarrassment)* Yes, my dear fellow, I know she's out. But where is she out?

LINGHAM *(moving left)* I don't know.

RICHARD There's nothing wrong, is there?

LINGHAM Well, she's not expecting you.

RICHARD Frances always expects me, Harold. That's the beautiful thing about my wife – who expects nothing except my presence. How long will she be?

LINGHAM *(sitting in the armchair left centre)* I do feel I should say something.

RICHARD Don't look so worried. Everything looks squeezed up inside you. Let go, expand and everything will be well. I'm never going away again. I'm going to take you all in hand, Harold. *(He turns around and surveys the room.)* First of all, I'm going to do up the place. You could do with a coat of paint yourself, and later – to work.

LINGHAM You're going back to the nylon shop?

**RICHARD** The nylon shop? Good grief, no. Big things, Harold. How is Sharpy? Did she find herself a man? You know, I always thought she might hook you, Harold.

**LINGHAM** Me?

**RICHARD** You could do a lot worse, Leaky-Jugs.

**LINGHAM** I was rather thinking of it from her point of view.

**RICHARD** You're not such a bad bargain, really. I'm sure she wouldn't mind a bit of mopping up. I like Sharpy. She feels the right things even if she never says them – and it's the heart that counts, Harold, and don't let those cold fishes with their eagle eyes tell you any differently. That's what I told Dr Creepy-Crawly-Cawley when he told me I had a hole inside me that had to be filled up. Do you know what I said to him, Harold? I said I'd appreciate it if he didn't use the same steel and concrete with which he'd filled up his own.

**LINGHAM** *(open-mouthed)* Then what happened?

**RICHARD** Old Nurse Robot says – *(he mimics her voice)* "Have a little self-control, Mr. Brough." "Not if it's going to get me where it got you, Nurse," I said. Ugh, these people who see right through you don't frighten us, do they, Harold?

**LINGHAM** No, Richard.

**RICHARD** Let's drink to that.

**LINGHAM** *(gulping)* Drink to it?

**RICHARD** *(roaring with laughter)* Don't look so frightened, Harold. I'm not a classified alcoholic. Just mildly schizophrenic – that's down on my card. No, just a toast, Harold, that's all.

**LINGHAM** But I don't think there's anything here.

**RICHARD** But I thought of that. *(He takes a bottle of gin from his pocket.)* Just one bottle, Harold, for the homecoming. *(He puts the bottle on the stool.)* Let's make the evening a party. How's my wonderful Henrietta?

FRANCES *enters by the front door. She carries a pair of long, white gloves.* LINGHAM *rises.*

*(he turns)* Frances!

FRANCES Richard!

RICHARD Well, at least she doesn't call me "Mr. Brough". Why are you all so open-mouthed? You were expecting me Monday, I come Sunday. Does a man have to give the exact hour of his arrival in his own house?

FRANCES *(crossing to* RICHARD *and hugging him)* Of course not. How are you?

RICHARD *(fervently)* I'm just glad to be home, Frances.

LINGHAM *(crossing to the door left)* I'll go to my room, if you'll excuse me.

RICHARD Don't bury yourself too deep, Harold. I shall come and dig you out later for the celebrations.

LINGHAM *exits left.*

FRANCES Celebrations?

RICHARD Well, you don't want to mourn me, do you? The dead aren't beckoning yet.

FRANCES Have you seen Ettie?

RICHARD Nope. Nobody here except Harold and his secret lantern, and now he's gone, it's our secret lantern. *(very seriously)* I'm all right, Fran – those bloody sweats have gone – and if they want to stare, let them stare. I'll damned well stare them out. The things I've got planned don't include them, anyway.

FRANCES Who, Richard?

RICHARD The Dr Cawleys and the law partners and any man who says, "It's all a matter of sticking the pin in where it hurts most before the other fellow does." My plans don't include them, Fran – only you and me. I've spewed up my pain and they can't get at me anymore.

**FRANCES** Who do you mean, Richard?

**RICHARD** *(impatiently)* Don't keep saying "Who?" The whole damn lot of them. *(He points to the lantern on the chest down centre.)* What is that?

**FRANCES** *does not answer.*

*(he turns to* **FRANCES***)* Why don't you answer me, Fran? I get the feeling you're not glad to see me – for the first time I get the feeling *you're* not glad I'm home. *(He picks up the bottle of gin and holds it aloft.)* I've quit this, Fran. I'm knitted up – I don't need it anymore. It's been rough, I know. The lousy little mats and the evening classes – and me and the sweats and all of it. But it's all over now and in six months I'm going to be a king and I'll pull you right up beside me where you belong. *(he pauses)* Say something, will you?

**FRANCES** I love you, Richard.

*They embrace. On the following speech,* **RICHARD***'s whole body tenses as though he is willing himself to believe the words.*

**RICHARD** You know, Dr Cawley says, "Take it easy and do what comes simply off my left hand." But I've got no time to crawl along on my belly, Frances – I've got to stride up there in one or two jumps and God help anybody who tries to stop me.

**FRANCES** *(gently)* No-one's going to stop you, Richard.

**RICHARD** They'll try.

**FRANCES** Who'll try, Richard?

**RICHARD** *(blinking his eyes)* The damn lot of them. Why are you dangling those gloves, Fran?

**FRANCES** I got them from Elsie. *(She moves above the table.)*

**RICHARD** *(with frustrated answer)* Is it such a crazy question and why are you screwing them up? *(He grabs the gloves and dangles them in his right hand.)* Long and formal. The room is full of these bloody exclusive objects. When I walk into my living-room, I say to myself, "Why is Leaky-Jugs dressing my home up like a Chinese whorehouse?", so I ask him what is that and he says "a lantern". *(he shouts violently)* I ask you, is that a proper answer to a proper question? I waited a long time to come home, Frances. *(He points to the lantern.)* What is that? *(He flings his arm over his eyes. He is almost at breaking point.)* What are these things that shut me out?

*The front door bell rings.*

*(He flings the gloves to the floor and turns up centre.)* Open it.

ELSIE *enters by the front door before* FRANCES *can move.* ELSIE *carries a pair of long, ivory gloves.*

ELSIE *(crossing to left of* FRANCES*)* I found a better pair, ivory – not dead white. Let's have a look at the dress and then you can match it against it.

FRANCES *indicates* RICHARD.

*(She turns and sees* RICHARD.*)* Oh! Oh, you gave me a proper turn.

RICHARD *smiles at* ELSIE, *but the insecurity which has touched him in the last few moments sours his words slightly.*

RICHARD Did they tell you I was dead, Sharpy? *(He capers across to* ELSIE.*)* Well, I am, and I've come back to haunt you at the nylon shop. Six pounds, eighteen shillings and a game of draughts with the employer and no questions asked. *(He winks at* ELSIE.*)*

ELSIE *(removing her wrap)* Are you better, Richard? *(She puts her wrap on the downstage arm of the sofa.)*

RICHARD *(slapping his stomach; still teasing)* Yes, they filled me up with concrete. *(He moves down centre.)*

ELSIE *moves to right of* RICHARD.

There's no room for gin. See. *(He opens his mouth wide.)* I'm solid all the way down.

FRANCES *crosses above the others, picks up the gloves and puts them on the footstool. For a moment,* ELSIE *is taken in and then realises* RICHARD *has been joking.*

ELSIE  Oh – oh, what a terrible man you are. But it is nice to see you. I bet you livened them up at – ah – that place.

RICHARD  Don't be a snob, Elsie. Call a spade a spade. *(He crosses and sits in the armchair left centre.)* Although I do like to think that I was a high-class misfit. *(He is beginning to flower again in this warming atmosphere.)*

ELSIE  *(moving centre)* I bet there wasn't one to touch you. Did you get in any games of draughts?

RICHARD  I threw it in after a couple of sessions with an ex-vicar. Every time he lost a game, he'd get up and murmur – *(he mimics the vicar's voice)* "He has deserted me, He has deserted me."

ELSIE  *(taking it quite literally)* What a poor loser. Well, you must tell me about it some other time. *(She turns to* FRANCES.*)* You two haven't seen each other for ages. *(She holds out the gloves.)* Try these with the dress and I'll have another hunt. *(She turns around and looks at the decorations.)* Oh, isn't that pretty. You have started early.

RICHARD *asks* ELSIE *a question quite simply, without shouting and without anger because he is absolutely sure of a truthful and direct answer.*

RICHARD  What is it, Sharpy?

ELSIE  *(turning to* RICHARD)* Decorations for the party, of course...

ELSIE *breaks off as* FRANCES *touches her arm.* ELSIE *is aware that she may have given away a surprise, but ignorant of the larger issue involved.*

*(she turns to* FRANCES.*)* Oh, I'm ever so sorry, Frances. It just popped out. Kick me, will you? I've always done it – and I had dozens of hidings as a kid for giving things away, but

I just can't stop. But I do feel mean, I've spoilt the surprise and Henrietta will never speak to me again.

FRANCES You run along, Elsie. I'll explain.

RICHARD *is determined not to let* ELSIE *go, aware that she alone by her very nature, cannot help but give him a direct answer.*

RICHARD No, *you* explain, Sharpy.

ELSIE Well, I'll have to tell him now I've gone this far, though I do think it was daft putting up the lanterns so soon. Why did you have to do it so soon when her birthday's not till Wednesday?

RICHARD Henrietta's birthday?

ELSIE *(turning to* RICHARD*)* Yes, but the party is really for you. A sort of surprise home-coming. I found them out because I could read it all over their faces that it was really for you.

RICHARD *rises and moves a step down left centre.*

FRANCES Elsie, *please.*

*It is too late.* RICHARD *is convinced that the party is for him, his anxiety drops and relief floods through him.*

RICHARD For me and Henrietta? A party? And now I've opened my big mouth and spoiled everything.

ELSIE No, it was my fault.

RICHARD *(turning to face* FRANCES*)* I've always got to know too much. I've no faith. Frances, forgive me.

FRANCES *(wildly)* Don't go on like this. Please, don't go on like this anymore.

ELSIE *(trying to be motherly)* Let's pretend nobody said anything. You can go on with the plans, just the same.

RICHARD You and Henrietta planned a party for me and I wrecked everything.

FRANCES Shut up, Richard. It's not like that, it's not like that at all.

ELSIE Why did you put up the decorations so soon? Decorations get ever so dusty.

RICHARD Don't tell Henrietta, Fran.

ELSIE *(conspiratorially)* It'll be our little secret.

RICHARD Let's have a drink to that.

FRANCES No, Richard, we will *not* drink to that.

RICHARD *(lightly)* Just orange juice, Fran. I'll get some glasses. *(He kisses* FRANCES *on the mouth.)* I'm a clumsy oaf, Fran. Try to forget it. *(He crosses to the kitchen door.)*

FRANCES *(following* RICHARD*)* Come back here, Richard.

RICHARD I'll just get the glasses.

RICHARD *exits to the kitchen.*

ELSIE *(crossing to the armchair left centre)* You do look upset. I'm terribly sorry. Don't take it so hard. Ettie won't know.

FRANCES *(turning to face* ELSIE*; unable to keep the secret any longer)* The party is *tonight*.

ELSIE *(not understanding)* Tonight? You weren't expecting him till Monday.

FRANCES *(deliberately)* That's why it was tonight.

ELSIE You didn't want him.

FRANCES That's right. We didn't want him.

ELSIE You're joking.

FRANCES No, I'm not joking, Elsie. I rang the home and asked them to keep him there till Monday. I'm afraid they let me down.

ELSIE But why?

FRANCES *(in agony and barely able to utter the words)* We thought he'd mess things up.

ELSIE But he's your husband.

FRANCES Yes, Elsie, he's my husband.

RICHARD *enters from the kitchen and stands framed in the doorway. His eyes are blinking and his fists are clenched tightly around three glasses.*

RICHARD The table is covered with food, Fran. Little bits of bread – strange little biscuits. Ones that come out at parties. *(He comes into the room, puts the glasses on the table then crosses below* FRANCES *to centre.)* You were eating a triangular biscuit when I first met you, Fran.

FRANCES *(moving to the bench left of the table)* You'd better go, Elsie.

RICHARD *(hysterically)* Don't keep pushing Elsie off. Elsie's all right. She hits the nail on the head. The trouble is, it's usually on the wrong bloody wall. Now, let's start from the beginning, shall we? *(He points to the lantern down centre.)* Elsie, what's that?

ELSIE *(nearly in tears)* A lantern – and I don't know any more, really I don't. It seems I've got it all wrong.

FRANCES Richard, stop it.

RICHARD *turns up centre.*

Let Elsie go home.

RICHARD *(wandering aimlessly around the stool)* Stale biscuits and dusty decorations and Dr Creepy-Crawly-Cawley trying to hold me like a leech *(he mimics)* "Stay till Monday, old boy. Heavy travelling on the weekend." Now, why should he want me to stay till Monday. He wouldn't get another twelve guineas because it's paid by the week. *(He speaks direct to* FRANCES, *with deliberate intent to hurt.)* You *do* pay it by the week, don't you, Fran? *(He moves to left of* FRANCES.*)*

FRANCES *I* pay it by the week.

RICHARD *(wincing)* Even that old electric shocking money-grabber wouldn't charge you for a few hours – so he was doing somebody a favour.

FRANCES  He was.

RICHARD  Who was he doing a favour, Fran?

ELSIE  *(now totally identified with* RICHARD*'s pain)* Don't tell
him, Fran. Don't hurt him.

FRANCES  Me. I asked him to keep you there till Monday.

ELSIE  Why did you have to say it? *(She sits in the armchair left
centre.)*

RICHARD  *(crying out in pain)* You wanted him to keep me there,
another day, another night in that *place?* You wanted to keep
me there when I could have been sweating in my own sheets.
Why, Fran, why?

FRANCES  So that Ettie could have her party.

RICHARD  Without me?

FRANCES  Yes.

RICHARD  Without me knowing? But that's damned silly. Harold
would have told me. Harold's my friend, he would have told
me. *(He rushes to the door left and flings it open.)* Harold,
were you going to this party? Were you?

LINGHAM *enters left.*

FRANCES  Harold's not concerned in this, Richard.

RICHARD  *(crossing to centre)* What do you mean – not concerned?
He was jollifying the place when I came in. Is that what you
thought, Harold? A jolly party without the master?

LINGHAM *stands mute.*

FRANCES  Harold just rents a room here. If you want him to go,
tell him.

RICHARD  So that's the trick, is it? *(He moves below the armchair
left centre.)* To tell me how I need you all. *(He points to
LINGHAM.)* You and your two pounds, twelve and six. *(He*

*points to* ELSIE.*)* And you and your nylon shop. *(He points to* FRANCES.*)* And you and your everlasting comfort.

ELSIE I wasn't invited. I thought it was Wednesday.

RICHARD *(turning to* ELSIE*)* Poor old Elsie. They thought you were a risk because you blab too much. *(He crosses above the armchair left centre to right of* LINGHAM.*)* But you don't blab, do you, Harold? Nice and quiet. The perfect little lodger. *(He moves above the armchair left centre.)* But I never thought you'd do this to me, Fran.

LINGHAM It wasn't her fault. It just all happened.

RICHARD What do you mean – happened? It was planned – every minute.

ELSIE I just don't get it. *(It is in this speech that she reveals her love for* RICHARD.*)* Why didn't you want him, why did you want a party without Richard?

HENRIETTA *enters quietly by the front door. Only* FRANCES *sees her.* HENRIETTA *stands in the open doorway, watching.*

RICHARD *(moving and standing above the left end of the chest down centre, facing front)* Why don't you answer the question, Fran? Why didn't you want me?

FRANCES Ask Henrietta.

RICHARD *turns and sees* HENRIETTA. *They stare at each other, animals from the jungle.* RICHARD's *fear is apparent. His eyes start to blink.* HENRIETTA *closes the door and crosses deliberately to right of* RICHARD.

HENRIETTA Ask me what? *(Her voice quivers a little, but she is in control.)* Hello, Father.

RICHARD's *anger has completely subsided.*

RICHARD Hello, Henrietta.

HENRIETTA Are you better?

RICHARD *(clenching his hands)* Yes, I'm better.

HENRIETTA *goes on talking, but underneath her calm there is a faintly hectic note.*

HENRIETTA We were going to have a special tea when you came home – on Monday or Tuesday. *(She turns and moves to left of* FRANCES.*)* Did you tell him about the special tea, Mother?

RICHARD *moves slowly up centre.* FRANCES, LINGHAM *and* ELSIE *are rooted in the atmosphere.*

FRANCES No.

HENRIETTA *(turning to* LINGHAM*)* Did you tell him, Mr. Lingham?

LINGHAM *(shakily)* No, I didn't.

HENRIETTA *(moving to right of* RICHARD*)* It was to have been a surprise. Mr. Lingham has another surprise, a book about birds.

RICHARD *picks up the bottle of gin and sits on the stool.*

Swallows. It has a wonderful cover.

RICHARD *(gulping)* Swallows, eh?

HENRIETTA The colour is beautiful. *(to* LINGHAM*)* Have you shown Father the book?

LINGHAM No, not yet, Ettie.

FRANCES *(moving to right of* HENRIETTA *and putting an arm around her; quietly)* Your father has just been here a little while, Ettie.

HENRIETTA Well, I'm sure he'd like to see it. *(She crosses towards the door left.)* It's green – a sort of jade. I'll get it.

ELSIE *(rising; unable to bear the tension any longer)* He knows – he knows, Ettie.

HENRIETTA *stands rigid.*

He looked at the lantern, and then he looked at me, and it just tumbled out.

HENRIETTA *(turning on* ELSIE*)* Tumbled out?

FRANCES About the party. Your father knows about the party. *(gently)* But it'll be all right, Ettie.

ELSIE *tries desperately to create an atmosphere of normality.*

ELSIE *(rising and looking at* HENRIETTA*)* Did you like the gloves?

LINGHAM She hasn't seen them yet, Miss Sharp.

ELSIE *(desperately)* I bet they'll look smashing. I hunted all over the shop for those gloves. I knew I had them somewhere.

RICHARD *removes the cap from the gin bottle and drops it on the floor.*

*(she turns to* LINGHAM*)* D'you know, they'd dropped behind the counter.

LINGHAM Really.

ELSIE Of course, the box was dirty...

HENRIETTA *(turning to* FRANCES*)* Where's the list?

ELSIE *(confused)* List – what for?

RICHARD You never ask what a list is for, Elsie. You take old Nurse Robot – she loves her lists. She's got lists up to the sky; and when she gives you her pill at night, she just ticks you off. *(he mimics)* "There's your pill, Mr. Brough, and now I'll just tick you off." *(He rises and drinks from the gin bottle.)* Oh, it's ever so simple. If somebody took away Nurse Robot's list she'd just disappear – a little cap and apron, standing all by themselves.

HENRIETTA I want that list. I can't remember the numbers.

ELSIE *(turning to* HENRIETTA*)* What numbers?

FRANCES You can't have it, Ettie. I won't give it to you.

**HENRIETTA** *runs across to the table.* **FRANCES** *quickly intercepts her, then takes the party list from the table drawer.*

**RICHARD** Robot loves numbers; she does everything by numbers. *(he mimics)*

"Mr. Brough, it's two

Now you spew.

Mr. Brough, it's four,

Sweat some more.

**HENRIETTA** *runs to the front door.*

Mr. Brough, it's five

What, still alive?"

**FRANCES** Richard, close your mouth. *(She turns to* **HENRIETTA.***)* Where are you going, Ettie?

**HENRIETTA** To stand at the door.

**FRANCES** Don't send them away, Ettie.

**HENRIETTA** I'll stand at the door all night, but I won't let them in.

**FRANCES** Please – you can't send them away.

**HENRIETTA** You got me into this, now you get me out.

**FRANCES** *(frantically)* What can I do?

**RICHARD** We'll have to paint Elsie with spots.

**ELSIE** *moves uneasily behind* **LINGHAM.**

She'll have to walk up and down outside, painted with little red spots.

**FRANCES** Can't you see what you're doing, Ettie?

**HENRIETTA** Would you let them in – in *here*?

**FRANCES** *(breaking)* Here, take it. *(She hands the list to* **HENRIETTA.***)*

RICHARD *(crossing to the table)* Harold can walk with Elsie and ring a bell.

HENRIETTA *runs to the bookshelves left and picks up the telephone.*

There was a little bell over here. *(He picks up the bell from the table.)* Oh, here we are. *(He moves down centre, ringing the bell.)*

HENRIETTA *carries the telephone to the chest down centre and comes face to face with* RICHARD. RICHARD *stops ringing the bell and drops it.*

FRANCES *(moving quickly between* RICHARD *and* HENRIETTA*)* Oh, don't look at her, Richard.

HENRIETTA *puts the telephone on the chest down centre, sits beside it and lifts the receiver.*

*(She holds* RICHARD's *arm.)* Don't, don't look at her, Richard, look at me.

HENRIETTA *dials a number.*

RICHARD *(breaking from* FRANCES*)* Quiet, everybody.

FRANCES *turns away and faces up centre.*

Quiet as mice, blind mice.

HENRIETTA There isn't anyone coming. There isn't anyone coming to the phone.

RICHARD *(bending over and facing* HENRIETTA*)* They'll come, when they've washed their teeth and they've brushed their hair, they'll come.

HENRIETTA *(into the telephone)* Hello, Mrs. Verney. Is Alison there? ...Thank you. Good-bye. *(She replaces the receiver.)* She's gone out. *(She looks fiercely at* RICHARD, *lifts the receiver and dials another number.)*

FRANCES *turns to* RICHARD, *takes his arm and turns him to face up centre.*

LINGHAM *(moving down left centre)* Why don't you go and lie down, Mr. Brough?

ELSIE *(moving to* RICHARD*)* Everyone feels better in the morning.

ELSIE *is right of* RICHARD, FRANCES *is left of him.*

HENRIETTA *(into the telephone)* Paula? ...Is Alison with you? ... She's not? ...

ELSIE *and* FRANCES *lead* RICHARD *towards the hall.*

Well, I rang up to say there isn't a party... Well, that's all, there isn't a party. *(She replaces the receiver.)*

LINGHAM *moves to the door left.* HENRIETTA *lifts the receiver and dials another number.*

RICHARD Where are you going, Harold?

LINGHAM Just to my room, Mr. Brough.

RICHARD What for, Harold? To look at the moon underneath your hyacinth bulb? It's well hidden, Harold, they can't get your moon.

FRANCES *and* ELSIE *attempt to draw* RICHARD *to the stairs.*

HENRIETTA *(into the telephone)* Jean, this is Ettie... Are you calling for Beryl? ...

RICHARD They can't get the vicar's moon, either.

HENRIETTA *(into the telephone)* Who else are you calling for? ...

RICHARD Over two years he's been in the home.

HENRIETTA *(into the telephone)* The party's off...

RICHARD Sixteen shocks he's had, and old Creepy-Crawly-Cawley can't get his moon. He must keep it in a very secret place.

HENRIETTA *(into the telephone)* I can't explain. There just can't be a party. *(She replaces the receiver.)*

RICHARD *breaks free and sends* ELSIE *and* FRANCES *flying.* HENRIETTA *lifts the receiver and dials another number.*

**RICHARD** The vicar and me, we'd be having a game in the evening, and old Dr Cawley would walk by, and the vicar'd bend his thin grey head across the table and whisper –

**FRANCES** *seizes her opportunity, takes the gin bottle from* **RICHARD** *and puts it on the table.*

– "Brough, he's worried, because he can't shock the moon out of me. He can pour in his voltage, but he can't shock the moon out."

**HENRIETTA**, *in her haste, has misdialled and tries again.*

Something tough about a man who can withstand all that electricity.

**FRANCES** *grabs* **RICHARD** *by his left arm and* **ELSIE** *takes his right arm. They pull him towards the stairs.*

**LINGHAM** *exits left.*

Where are we going, Frances?

**ELSIE** You're going to lie down, Richard.

**RICHARD** Lying down's no different from standing up. Ceilings are just rearranged walls, Elsie. Shut in a box, you're just shut in a box.

**HENRIETTA** *(into the telephone)* Hello, Elizabeth, this is Ettie...

**RICHARD** *(suddenly moving to the stairs)* Nail me up, Frances. Nail me up.

**RICHARD** *runs up the stairs and exits.*

**FRANCES** *and* **ELSIE** *follow him rapidly off.* **HENRIETTA** *is alone.*

**HENRIETTA** *(into the telephone)* I'm calling to cancel the party... Someone is ill.

*Curtain.*

# ACT II

## Scene One

*Scene – the same. Later the same evening.*

*When the curtain rises, the stage is empty. The lights are on, but the lanterns and candles are out.* **LINGHAM** *enters left and crosses above the armchair left centre to centre. The rattle of a tea cup is heard off up the stairs.* **LINGHAM** *beats a hasty retreat and exits left.* **ELSIE** *enters down the stairs, carrying a supper tray. She pauses at the kitchen door, then crosses to centre with the tray.*

**ELSIE** *(calling)* Mr. Lingham?

**LINGHAM** *appears at the door left.*

Frances doesn't want it. Would you like something?

**LINGHAM** No, I'm not really hungry. I feel as though I'll never have an appetite again. As though nothing will work quite right again. How are they?

**ELSIE** Frances is in bed. She looks awful and he's sitting in the spare room, fully dressed. He just told me to go away.

*ELSIE crosses and exits to the kitchen.* **LINGHAM** *comes into the room, closes the door and moves centre.*

*ELSIE re-enters from the kitchen.*

**LINGHAM** How's Henrietta?

**ELSIE** *(crossing to right of* **LINGHAM***)* Her light's out. There wasn't a sound. *(Bitterly)* How *can* she sleep?

**LINGHAM** You mustn't hate her. The nicest thing about you, Miss Sharp, is that you're not a bit like your name.

**ELSIE** She's a cold fish, Mr. Lingham. A cold fish. *(She leans on the back of the armchair above the table.)* The way she looked up all those numbers and rang all those people and told them the party's off made me sick – and he just come home. I couldn't bear to look at him.

**LINGHAM** You admire him very much.

**ELSIE** I think he's marvellous – a real man, that's what he is. Of course, he has his ups and downs but it couldn't be plain sailing for a man like that.

**LINGHAM** Like what?

**ELSIE** Well, a man with things to do. I used to think how lucky I was to know him. To be there, in the bad patch. *(She moves below the sofa.)* I knew it had to end, that some time he'd be off and it really used to depress me that I'd be stuck with somebody ordinary –

**LINGHAM** *(murmuring)* Yes.

**ELSIE** – after him. *(She sits on the sofa.)* I expect that's why I never married – although I had a few chances.

**LINGHAM** But you've only known him a few years.

**ELSIE** I've been waiting, I suppose. The others never had any size, if you know what I mean.

**LINGHAM** *(moving to the fireplace)* I know what you mean, Miss Sharp.

**ELSIE** When he gets hurt, he gets hurt big. I could never hurt him. Of course, I couldn't if I tried.

**LINGHAM** I enjoyed our game of draughts the other night.

**ELSIE** *(warmly)* So did I. I always felt you and I had that in common. *(She looks towards the top of the stairs.)*

**LINGHAM** Draughts?

ELSIE  No. Him.

LINGHAM  I enjoyed it because of you. I felt as though I had a
life of my own. We've never talked like this before. Am I
embarrassing you?

ELSIE  No, of course not.

LINGHAM  There isn't much size to me, is there?

ELSIE  *(sitting back and crossing her legs)* I wouldn't say that.

LINGHAM  No, everything is on a minor scale. I think if I tried to
do anything large, I might burst. But I did enjoy the draughts
and the ham.

ELSIE  I was so afraid you might hate ham – that you were just
being kind. *(She uncrosses her legs and leans forward to*
LINGHAM.*)* You must admit the beer was flat. We must do
it again.

LINGHAM  Have you ever thought what would happen to us if
things were all right here? If Richard didn't need the job
and the nylon shop and they didn't have to rent the room?

ELSIE  Then what would happen to us loose ends, is that what
you mean? I don't know, I've always been a loose end, really.
Curling my sister's hair so that she could catch a husband.
The shop's my own, but even that meant nothing till Richard
came. *(She breaks off, determined to break the line of thought,
rises and moves below the sofa.)* I'd better clear these things.
Shall we take the lanterns down? *(She stands on the stool.)* I
don't suppose he'll want to see them in the morning. *(She turns
on the stool and points to the lantern down centre.)* When he
pointed to it and said, "What's that, Elsie?" I could have died.
He'll never trust me anymore – or you. It's like everyone was
ganging up against him. *(with her hand to her heart)* But at
least, we *felt* it. She didn't even *feel* it. *(She gets down from the
stool.)* She just looked up those numbers. Why didn't she want
him at the party? What's wrong with him? *(She bursts into
tears and collapses on to the stool. She is so overcome that she*

*turns on* LINGHAM *and begins, for a moment, to attack him.)* You knew they were planning it. Why didn't *you* stop them?

LINGHAM *(moving up left of the stool)* I'm the wrong size, Elsie.

ELSIE You didn't say anything. You just stood there.

LINGHAM I get paralysed and I can't find out where I belong. You see, Miss Sharp, I've wandered around all my life. Never made any friends. No-one ever seemed to need anything. Then I met Mr. Brough. We were in a train. *(He crosses above the stool to right of it.)* Yes, I remember, it stopped at a station and he got out, and came back with some tea. *(still pleased at the thought)* D'you know, he bought one for me. And then he asked about a plant I had with me. He touched the leaves in such a gentle way, and the things I'd felt all my life he was suddenly voicing. Everything was so jolly, and when we got out, we walked through the station as though we had always been friends. *(He sits on the sofa.)* Then we had eggs and chips at a small café, and I quite forgot that my landlady had prepared supper. *(still apologetic for this break in routine)* It was just a cold supper, you know, so it really didn't matter. And then he told me about the room. When I walked home that night I had quite decided to come here.

ELSIE *(turning to* LINGHAM*)* Because he made you so happy.

LINGHAM Partly. Well, this seems silly, but because I thought that some day I might be able to do something for him.

ELSIE But we can't do anything, can we? *(she rises)* I'm sorry, I didn't mean to hurt you. I just can't bear to think of her sleeping up there and him sitting in that room and I can't help him.

LINGHAM *(rising)* You could help *me*, but I suppose that wouldn't be the same.

ELSIE *(surprised)* Help you? But you're so quiet. I wouldn't know what to say. *(She sits on the stool, facing* LINGHAM.*)*

LINGHAM Well, if I could pop into the shop sometimes.

ELSIE Of course you can. You know how I love a little chat. Richard and me, we'd close it up dead on one o'clock. That hour till two o'clock was the best I'd ever had. Him joking about the customers, drinking his beer – what a swallow he's got. "Elsie," he'd say, "we'll never get rich like this. We're enjoying ourselves too much." *(She cries and turns away left on the stool.)*

LINGHAM *crosses above the stool to left of it.*

And sometimes when he'd arrive in the morning, he'd look all grey and tired and I'd know that something had gone on here, but I'd never dare ask, but always – on his worst days – he'd say, "I've got a wonderful daughter, Elsie." *(She rises and turns on* LINGHAM.*)* What went on over here?

LINGHAM Nothing.

ELSIE No rows? *(She looks, up the stairs.)* God, I could have hit her when she looked right through him as if he didn't exist. *(She looks front.)* No woman ought to look at a man like that. *(She breaks off, turns to* LINGHAM *and smiles.)* Oh, I'm off again. And you wanted me to help you. *(She giggles, turns away and sits on the sofa at the downstage end.)* What exactly was it you wanted?

LINGHAM *(with a step towards her)* I've never been able to bring it out.

ELSIE Go on, try, and don't worry. I've heard people ask for some funny things in my time.

LINGHAM *(with lowered eyes; shyly)* I've always wanted *company* of my own.

ELSIE You mean somebody to visit?

LINGHAM Do you know why I like the pigeons?

ELSIE Well, they're quite nice, really.

LINGHAM They don't ask too much of me. I'd like somebody around who'd *mind* and who didn't ask too much of me. I'd be afraid of letting them down.

ELSIE  You wouldn't let anyone down.

LINGHAM  I did, tonight. I should have done something.

ELSIE  *(trying to comfort him)* I suppose it wasn't your business.

LINGHAM  It *was* my business. I was his friend. You said yourself, I just stood there.

ELSIE  I was just blabbering on. My mouth talks a lot of rubbish all by itself sometimes and I don't mean a word of it. Richard used to say... *(She breaks off.)* I keep harping on it, don't I? Don't take any notice, I'll get over it. I've just got it on my mind tonight. *(she rises)* Probably I'm making a big fuss about nothing. What were you saying about your pigeons?

LINGHAM  Nothing.

ELSIE  *(trying to be bright)* Do you know what we ought to do? *(She points at the draughts on the footstool.)* We ought to go and have a game.

LINGHAM  Do you think so? Do you think that's right.

ELSIE  Well, there's nothing right about hanging round here, that's for certain. Isn't it better to try and cheer each other up? *(She moves to the hall.)* Now, get the board.

LINGHAM  Well, if you're really sure.

ELSIE  *(now in full command)* Go on, get it. *(She gets her wrap and* LINGHAM*'s hat and coat from the hall.)*

LINGHAM *smiles at* ELSIE *and collects the draughts box and board from the footstool.*

You wanted some company, didn't you? *(She gives* LINGHAM *his hat.)*

LINGHAM *puts the draught box and board with his hat on the stool.*

Come on, let's go. *(She helps* LINGHAM *on with his coat.)*

RICHARD *appears on the stairs, sees* ELSIE *and* LINGHAM *and hastily withdraws.*

*(She puts on her wrap.)* You know, I don't think I've got a thing in the place. We could take something from here, I suppose. *(She goes into the hall.)*

**LINGHAM** *picks up the draughts and his hat and follows* **ELSIE**.

No, perhaps that's not such a good idea. Let's try and rustle up something of our own.

**LINGHAM** *and* **ELSIE** *exit quietly by the front door.*

**RICHARD** *enters down the stairs. He is fully dressed and carries his suitcase. He moves to the table and picks up the bottle of gin. The front door bell rings.* **RICHARD** *puts the bottle in his pocket, moves to the front door and slowly opens it.*

**SOYA** *enters by the front door.*

**RICHARD** Hello.

**SOYA** Hello.

**RICHARD** What's the time?

**SOYA** *(starting to remove his coat)* About eleven o'clock. I suppose I'm too late for the party. *(He peers into the room.)* Nobody here?

**RICHARD** There's me, but I'm just going.

**SOYA** I was expected earlier but I've been walking around. I didn't think it would break up before twelve but it's just as well it's all finished. Now I don't have to bother to explain. *(He starts to put on his coat.)* Goodnight. *(He turns to go.)*

**RICHARD** *(grabbing* **SOYA***'s arm)* What did you say about explaining?

**SOYA** Just that I'm sick of it.

**RICHARD** *(moving into the room)* Come in and have a drink. *(He puts his case under the table.)*

**SOYA** *removes his coat and hangs it in the hall.*

**SOYA** *(coming into the room)* Anything left?

**RICHARD** *(taking the bottle from his pocket and holding it up)* This is personal property.

**SOYA** *(moving to right of* **RICHARD***)* Do you always bring your own?

**RICHARD** Well, it's good to have a spare.

**SOYA** What is it?

**RICHARD** Gin. You like it?

**SOYA** Never tried. Pour me one. What does it matter, anyway? I'm not going home anymore and I can't do anymore explaining.

**RICHARD** *pours two drinks.*

**RICHARD** Well, knock it back. *(He sits in the armchair above the table.)*

**SOYA** *drinks the gin in one swallow and coughs.*

**SOYA** It's horrible.

**RICHARD** Don't worry, you can't taste the third. *(He drains his glass.)*

**SOYA** Well, you'd better give me the second one, quick. I could have done with this yesterday.

**RICHARD** *pours two more drinks.*

The minute I saw the questions I knew I failed. *(He drinks.)*

**RICHARD** *(looking up)* Failed what?

**SOYA** Oh, sorry. The exam. Engineering – I think. You know, for years I've been trying to push that stuff into my brain and I still don't know what it's for. I just keep hearing Ettie saying, "You will, you will."

**RICHARD** Henrietta Brough?

**SOYA** *(grinning)* Only her dad calls her "Henrietta".

**RICHARD** Sit down.

**SOYA** *sits on the upstage end of the bench right of the table.*

**SOYA** Imagine a dwarf like me saying "Henrietta". Do you know her well?

**RICHARD** No. Tell me about the exam.

**SOYA** If you don't know the answers, you can't manufacture them. 'Cause it's got to be the same answer everybody else gives. I looked around the exam room and I knew by their faces, they were all in accord. All scribbling the same little numbers. Then I looked at the chap in charge, the one that sits at the desk. Do you know what the look in his eyes said? It said, "I know you're a goat amongst all these nice little baaing sheep. Go home, you don't belong." And I felt like saying, "Well, goats know a few things that sheep haven't learned yet. And was it *my* fault I'd been put in a wrong field and had he ever seen a goat under a car?"

**RICHARD** And what did he say?

**SOYA** Oh, I didn't tell him any of those things. What do you do?

**RICHARD** I'm a bookkeeper.

**SOYA** Figures. You see, to really amount to anything, you've got to have the figures, otherwise, where are you?

**RICHARD** Tell me.

**SOYA** You're under a car, stinking of grease and messing up the lounge. Avoiding Mother's friends. You know, it's better to be dead than under a car. Dead, you can't embarrass anybody. How do you feel about overalls? I bet they give you the creeps. You, a bookkeeper.

**RICHARD** Overalls terrify me.

**SOYA** You're kidding.

**RICHARD** The men that wear them have glinty blue eyes and brown fingers that know how the whole world works. Like

Martians to some, that's overalls to me. Dominant, purposeful and really in control.

**SOYA** Gosh, I wish my dad felt like that – or Ettie.

**RICHARD** What does Henrietta say?

**SOYA** Something about fleets of cars going all by themselves. I just want *one* car to fix. Does that make any sense?

**RICHARD** *nods.*

*(he leans forward, elbows on the table)* You wouldn't think someone wanting to fix cars could drive anyone crazy. I'd really made up my mind to tell Dad that me and big business just wouldn't get along, and then I met Ettie and I tried her with the overalls.

**RICHARD** Is this why you've been walking around?

**SOYA** If you just don't know the answers, you just don't know the answers, and she's such a wonderful girl. I just can't tell her I've failed. I tried to explain the things I wanted to do but she just kept putting me up in this tower, where I control all these cars.

**RICHARD** *reacts and leans forward on the table.*

Do you know about that?

**RICHARD** *(flatly)* Yes, I know all about that.

**SOYA** Do you think I could do it?

**RICHARD** Control all the cars in Ettie's head?

**SOYA** No, make it come true without the exams.

**RICHARD** So that she can pay off with a look of everlasting respect in her eyes. That's what you're looking for, isn't it? The look of everlasting respect in her eyes. Believe me, I know all about that.

**SOYA** Are you drunk?

**RICHARD** Answer the question.

**SOYA** I'm just sick of being nothing.

**RICHARD** First you complain because your father wants to make you over and then you come right over here and toy with the idea of letting Ettie remodel you. Aren't you just somebody?

**SOYA** No.

**RICHARD** Shall I tell you what nothing is? Nothing's up in that bloody tower, trying to squeeze yourself into Ettie's favourite shape.

**SOYA** Oh, I don't take that stuff seriously about towers. It's just a game. Ettie wants me to be something. You see, her father does research.

**RICHARD** *(leaning back)* Research into what?

**SOYA** Well, I don't know exactly.

**RICHARD** You don't know anything, son, except how to fix a car. Why don't you go fix it?

**SOYA** What do you do when everyone's expecting things you can't give them?

**RICHARD** You give yourself something.

**SOYA** You mean the overalls.

**RICHARD** Yes.

**SOYA** Well, I've got them, in a way.

**RICHARD** Don't hide them – hang them out the window.

**SOYA** *(leaning back)* You *are* drunk.

**RICHARD** Hang them out of the window with "This is me" written on them in bold, big print.

   **SOYA** *sniggers.*

   Why do you laugh?

**SOYA** I was thinking of my father's face with these things hanging out of the window. Have you ever told Ettie what you think about her?

**RICHARD** Told her – told her what?

**SOYA** You really sound as if you hate her.

**RICHARD** Don't talk rubbish. *(He refills his glass.)*

**SOYA** Do you really like that stuff?

**RICHARD** *drinks.*

**RICHARD** Sometimes I fall in love with it.

**SOYA** When I feel bad, I cut out engines. Why don't you try that?

**RICHARD** It's too late, I thought of gin first. *(He turns on* **SOYA**.*)* But do you think if I had *one* car to fix...

**SOYA** Don't keep harping on it. I can't do it. *(he shrugs)* Don't worry, I'll think of something. I've got a few plans. If you know all the answers, why do you keep guzzling that stuff? *(he holds up the bottle)* You ought to hang this out of your window with "This is me" written in bold, large print. *(He puts down the bottle.)*

**RICHARD** *winces, then grins.*

**RICHARD** It's a deal. If you hang the overalls, I'll hang this.

**SOYA** *(admiringly)* I believe you would.

**RICHARD** *grins.*

*(he leans forward)* How did you get to know Ettie?

**RICHARD** The question is, how did Henrietta get to know me? With her special eye.

**SOYA** Yes, she really understands.

**RICHARD** She understands nothing. She just sees through you. There's quite a difference.

**SOYA** What does she see?

RICHARD  Not much, but enough. In me, a big hole and in you, a small doubt and it's that *doubt* she's after. When you met Henrietta what did you think?

SOYA  Well, I...

RICHARD  *(interrupting)* I'll tell you. *(he leans forward)* You thought – *(he speaks as* SOYA*)* "I'm not good enough so I'll whip myself a little." You won't have to do it for long, son. She'll soon take the whip and do it for you and eventually you'll fall in a sewer – and will she nurse your poor mangled head? No, she'll bury you quick because Henrietta can't stand the sight of blood.

SOYA  *(beginning to be suspicious)* Who invited you to this party?

RICHARD  *(roaring with laughter)* Invited me? Invited *me*? Boy, the foundations shook when I walked in.

SOYA  You weren't invited.

RICHARD  Invited? The walls fell in and only Henrietta was calm. Leaky-Jugs dithered and Elsie just whimpered and Fran looked away, but Henrietta came to the fundamental point of saving her own skin. That girl really knows the answers when it comes to survival. My God, she's had to do with me around.

*The telephone rings.* RICHARD *rises, crosses to the telephone and lifts the receiver.*

*(into the telephone)* Hello? ...Yes? ... *(He turns to* SOYA.*)* What's your name?

SOYA  Marshall, Soya Marshall.

RICHARD  It's your father.

SOYA *rises, takes a quick swig of gin, crosses and takes the receiver from* RICHARD *who moves below the armchair left chair.*

SOYA  *(into the telephone)* Hello...

HENRIETTA *enters on the stairs, and comes slowly down, listening.*

Yes... What? ...Yes... How did you know? ...Well, I'll tell you when I come home. I'm just talking to someone... 'Bye. *(He replaces the receiver and turns to* RICHARD.*)* He says there wasn't any party. Someone rang up to say it was cancelled. Was it cancelled because of you?

RICHARD  Yes, because of me.

SOYA  Why didn't you tell me?

HENRIETTA  Was that the phone?

RICHARD *turns and stares at* HENRIETTA.

RICHARD  It was Mr. Marshall's father to tell him the party's cancelled and to ask him about the exam.

HENRIETTA  *(coming into the room)* Hadn't you better go to bed?

RICHARD  *(crossing below* HENRIETTA *to the hall)* Yes, I'd better go to bed.

HENRIETTA  *(turning to* SOYA*)* How long have you been here?

SOYA  *(crossing to left of* HENRIETTA*)* I don't know. We've been talking.

HENRIETTA  Talking? I waited until ten. I didn't think you'd come.

RICHARD *moves up the stairs.*

*(she turns to* RICHARD*)* Good night.

RICHARD  Goodnight, Henrietta. *(He stops half way up the stairs.)*

HENRIETTA  *(turning to* SOYA*)* Well, how did it go, Soya?

SOYA  *(turning away)* What?

RICHARD  The exam. She wants to know about the exam.

HENRIETTA  *(turning to* RICHARD*)* Go to bed. This isn't anything to do with you.

RICHARD  All right. I shouldn't have talked to him.

HENRIETTA  You talked? *(She tries not to betray herself and her desperate hope that nothing damaging has come out.)*

**SOYA** We talked our heads off.

**HENRIETTA** *(turning to* **SOYA***)* But what happened yesterday?

**SOYA** Well, when I got on to the train, I was really optimistic.

**HENRIETTA** I told you.

**SOYA** And all through the exam, I did just like you said. I kept you running through my head, all the time.

**RICHARD** But you couldn't tell him the answers.

**HENRIETTA** *(turning and moving towards the stairs)* Will *you* please go to bed. *You* don't know anything about this.

**SOYA** That's not true, Ettie.

> **HENRIETTA** *turns to* **SOYA***.*

I told him about the exams. I had a few gins.

**HENRIETTA** *(whirling to face the stairs)* You gave him gin?

**SOYA** Well, it wasn't like that, Ettie. I felt like lead, walking around.

**HENRIETTA** *(facing front)* Why didn't you come straight here?

**SOYA** I was afraid to tell you.

**HENRIETTA** *(moving to right of* **SOYA***)* Tell me?

**SOYA** That I've failed.

**HENRIETTA** *(facing front; shattered)* I don't believe it. You couldn't fail. *(She tries quickly to cover it up.)* And even if you have, it's just a *silly* exam. Who needs a lot of silly numbers, anyway, *bits* of paper *cluttering* up the drawers. You don't need *bits* of paper saying you are somebody. You *are* somebody.

**SOYA** You really believe that?

> **RICHARD** *comes down the stairs to right of* **HENRIETTA***.*

*(he looks at* **RICHARD***)* You see, you're wrong, she really believes in me.

**HENRIETTA** *(turning to* **RICHARD***)* Are you still there?

RICHARD Yes, I'm still here.

HENRIETTA You must be tired. Why don't you go and rest?

RICHARD *(moving to the stairs)* Yes, I'll go and rest.

SOYA *(crossing above* HENRIETTA *to* RICHARD *and grabbing his arm)* What is this? Why don't you tell her what you said?

HENRIETTA Said?

SOYA About the tower, about how it's not a game.

RICHARD Oh, I talk a lot of rubbish when I've been drinking. Never listen to me. The things I say.

HENRIETTA That's right. He just rambles on.

> *At this moment, both* RICHARD *and* HENRIETTA *are united in their effort to preserve the fantasy, but* SOYA *breaks it.*

SOYA *(drawing* RICHARD *back into the room)* He was *not* rambling on. *(To* RICHARD*)* You said, "If you had one car you really wanted to fix..."

HENRIETTA Leave him alone. Can't you see he's worn out?

SOYA Worn out nothing. He was fine until you walked down the stairs. I was beginning to believe him.

HENRIETTA *(crossing below* SOYA *to left of* RICHARD*; losing control)* *Father*, go to bed. *Please* go to bed. *(She collapses into the armchair above the table, leaning forward on her hands.)*

SOYA *(moving to left of* HENRIETTA*)* Why do you keep trying to get rid of him? *(He suddenly realises what* HENRIETTA *has called* RICHARD*.)* What did you call him?

RICHARD *(moving to right of* HENRIETTA*)* He didn't know, Henrietta.

HENRIETTA *(sitting up and facing front)* You didn't know?

SOYA He's your father?

HENRIETTA You didn't know?

**SOYA** How would I know? Why did you tell me all that stuff? All that stuff about research?

**RICHARD** You mustn't take everything so literally.

    **SOYA** *moves centre then turns to* **RICHARD**, *horrified by the change which has taken place in him.*

**SOYA** Well, what about the car – about *one* car? How I should really believe in it?

    **RICHARD** *crosses above* **HENRIETTA** *to left of her and takes her hand.*

**RICHARD** One car? A dozen cars. Things can grow, can't they?

**SOYA** But that's not what you said. *(he breaks off)* Do you *remember* what you said?

**RICHARD** More or less. You're not going to check me word for word, are you? I know I thought you were a fine boy – yes, a very nice boy, with a big future. I spotted that all right, the moment I saw you at the door. I knew you were going to do big things.

**SOYA** *(horrified) Big things?* You invited me in because I'd *failed* the exam.

    **RICHARD** *stares in front of him, and the furtive words come out. He trips over them, trying to give them some semblance of sense.*

**RICHARD** Oh, that's right, yes – the exam. Er, well, er, not everybody needs exams, I mean, some detour, that's right, they bypass...

**SOYA** *(desperately)* But we talked – you really talked to me. Why didn't you say you were Ettie's father?

**RICHARD** Well, er, I don't think it came up.

**SOYA** Didn't come *up?* You speak as though we just said, "How do you do?" I was ready to go home and fling the mud about. I was ready to walk right into the lounge and say, "I met a man who said the overalls are all right, and I believe him."

RICHARD I'll just sit down. *(He sits on the sofa.)*

SOYA *(turning to* HENRIETTA*)* That's what he said, and I believed him.

HENRIETTA *rises, crosses below* SOYA *to the armchair left centre and sits.*

That sick feeling I had when I thought of facing my father – and that sick feeling I had when I thought of facing you, Ettie – it went away. When I walked through that door tonight, it went away – and I don't know why you're not answering me, Ettie, or why you're not speaking to him, and I don't know what I'm going to do or anything – but the towers are too much for me. *(He crosses to the hall and collects his coat.)* They're just too much for me. *(He crosses to* RICHARD.*)* Well, thank you for the drink, Mr. Brough. I'd better go home, now. *(He stands in agonised silence.)* Haven't you got anything to say to him, Ettie? Speak to him, Ettie, please.

HENRIETTA Will I see you again?

SOYA No, don't say that, Ettie. Speak to your father.

HENRIETTA Will I?

SOYA *rushes out by the front door, slamming it behind him.*

*(she turns on* RICHARD, *full of terrified rage)* Well, what did you tell him?

RICHARD Nothing.

HENRIETTA I *saw* his face – the way he looked at me. *(desperately)* What did you tell him about *us*?

RICHARD *(falteringly)* I – I gave him a drink – a chat – a little comfort – he was afraid.

HENRIETTA He talked of the towers – what did you tell him about the towers?

RICHARD *(shaking his head)* I didn't tell him, he found out.

HENRIETTA *(fearfully)* What did he find?

RICHARD A cold place, Henrietta – a place for living corpses.

HENRIETTA *(looking around the room)* Here? *(She looks at* RICHARD, *then at herself.)* Us? Freaks? Is that it? You told him we were freaks?

RICHARD *(quietly)* He cuts out engines.

HENRIETTA I've got to call him back. I've got to tell him that *it's you – you* that's full of shrieks in the night.

RICHARD He knows all about me, Ettie.

HENRIETTA *(staring at him)* Does he? What does he know? Does he know that you suck up gin and spit out slime and that you want to cover me with it – that you came into my room at nights and pulled out the eyes of a teddy-bear and said, "A blind bear is a happier bear"? *(She rises and moves slowly centre.)* How you caught me in corners till I squeezed up so small I nearly disappeared – and when you couldn't trap me in your arms they carried you off to a home – did you tell him *that*? How no-one but I knew that you crouched behind your jokes, waiting to grab me?

RICHARD *(rising)* To hold you, Henrietta – *(he moves towards* HENRIETTA, *with outstretched arms)* to hold you.

HENRIETTA *(backing to the armchair left centre)* Don't touch me. You grew out of the ground wherever I walked and when there was quiet, I could hear you breathing in every part of the house – at night, I could hear you listening at my door – breathing – why were you listening?

RICHARD For the sound of your heart.

HENRIETTA *(crouching in the armchair left centre)* Don't come near me.

RICHARD So you built a tower and hid from me.

HENRIETTA And I'll hide the rest of my life, but you'll never come near me.

**RICHARD** *(moving centre)* You've got to come down, Henrietta, you'll die up there, Henrietta. *That's* what he found out, Henrietta – why the sleek grey cars go all by themselves – because the drivers are dead and you'd have slaughtered that boy.

**HENRIETTA** It's you who killed everything – look at my mother...

**RICHARD** Don't say that, Henrietta. What do you know of love – you'd hear that boy cry in the night and you'd step on that lovely sound, which is the only thing that really makes him "somebody".

**HENRIETTA** It's your cry I'd stamp on – that ugly, squawking with flapping wings – what do I know of love? *(She rises and moves to left of* **RICHARD.***)* What do you know? Is it my mother? Is it Elsie or Harold? You didn't want them – only I knew what you really wanted – only I knew.

**RICHARD** *stares at* **HENRIETTA,** *then he grabs her, shakes her firmly then pushes her into the armchair left chair.*

**HENRIETTA** *rises, backs up centre, then runs out by the front door, slamming it behind her.*

**RICHARD** Ettie, my little girl. Where's my little girl?

*Curtain.*

## Scene Two

*Scene – the same. Early the following morning.*

*When the curtain rises the lights are on.* RICHARD *is lying huddled up, fully dressed, under a rug on the sofa. The gin bottle lies empty on the floor beside the sofa. After a few moments,* RICHARD *stirs, rubs his eyes, and sits bolt upright, his body rigid with fear. He stares at his hands and rubs the sweat from the palms and breathes deeply. He rises, not noticing the rug, which slips to the floor. He staggers out to the kitchen and re-enters a few seconds later, carrying a glass of Alka-Seltzer. He sits in the armchair above the table.* FRANCES *enters down the stairs. She is dressed. Her face is pale and exhausted. Her hands are clenched as though she is trying with her last dregs of energy to hold things together. She stares at* RICHARD.

FRANCES Richard. Why are you up so early? It's only half past seven. You look so tired. *(She notices the dishevelled sofa and the rug.)* You slept down here?

RICHARD *(abruptly)* That's right.

FRANCES *(moving and picking up the rug)* But I thought you were in the spare room. I saw the light on.

RICHARD I was going to leave last night, Fran. At least, I kidded myself I was going to. But I stayed, with the first damned excuse that was offered me.

FRANCES *(moving to* RICHARD *and folding the rug)* Leave?

RICHARD I was going back to Cawley – I was going to beg him to cut my heart out.

FRANCES What changed your mind?

RICHARD We had a night visitor. A boy – a nice boy, Fran. They've got him. He's all churned up and in a mess.

FRANCES Was it Soya Marshall?

RICHARD Yes.

FRANCES Richard, does Ettie know you met him? Does she know?

RICHARD *pauses and blinks his eyes.*

RICHARD No. She was in bed.

FRANCES *(putting the rug on the sofa)* I'd better call Harold. It's getting late. *(She opens the window curtains up right centre.)*

RICHARD What are you going to do, Frances? Watch the clock, go on with daily living?

FRANCES *crosses and opens the window curtains up left.*

That's it, isn't it, you've made up your mind to go on. Well, this isn't a matter of minds, Frances. You've got to say something to me. You're my wife.

FRANCES *(turning to RICHARD)* Am I?

RICHARD Well, of course you are.

FRANCES *(moving to the sofa)* I've got to call Harold. *(She picks up the rug and bottle.)* I've got to get breakfast and I've got to go to work. *(She goes to the hall and switches off the lights.)*

RICHARD Stop blinding me with facts. Maybe you're disappointed that I didn't leave last night. With me safely locked up with Cawley, you could go on with your nice comfortable facts.

FRANCES *(turning to face him)* They are not comfortable, Richard, but they are all I have.

RICHARD You'd better call Harold.

FRANCES You call him; I'm going to make breakfast.

FRANCES *exits to the kitchen.* RICHARD *rises, crosses to the door left and, taps it gently.*

RICHARD Harold? Harold? It's getting late, Leaky-Jugs. Harold, are you in there?

LINGHAM *enters left, crosses and sits on the stool. He is fully dressed.*

*(He moves to left of* LINGHAM.*)* Why, Harold, all dressed up. *(confidentially)* Did you hear us at it – Fran and me? Silly, isn't it? Things don't change much, do they, Harold? *(the bravado comes back into his voice)* This beating each other up has got to stop. We've all got to settle down. Well, I suppose it was a bit of a shock, my popping up like that, but you've digested me now, haven't you?

LINGHAM *is silent.*

*(He winks broadly at* LINGHAM.*)* Or am I too tough? You know, the best thing is to swallow me in one piece. *(*LINGHAM*'s silence is beginning to unnerve him and he tries to reassure himself.)* Poor old Harold's not awake, and me barraging him with friendship at seven-thirty in the morning. *(He taps* LINGHAM *on the knee.)* Well, he's still working. *(He can wait no longer for comfort.)* Come on, Leaky-Jugs. Say something.

LINGHAM  I'm going away, Mr. Brough.

RICHARD *does not hear the sentence.*

RICHARD  *(laughing)* Mr. Brough? Mr. Brough? I thought we'd had all that out, Harold. Now try it: "Richard".

LINGHAM  *(quietly)* I'm going away. I'm going away.

RICHARD  *(dazed)* Clearing out?

LINGHAM  I'm sorry it's such short notice, but I'm sure Mrs. Brough will have no trouble letting such a comfortable room.

RICHARD, *feeling surrounded by enemies, moves below the sofa and calls belligerently towards the kitchen.*

RICHARD  Hey, Fran, come in here. I've found you a factual friend. You can add up your pennies together. Harold's clearing out and wants to settle his account. He wants things nice and tidy. *(he turns)* That's what you all want, isn't it? To sweep the crumbs under the carpet. "No-one can say we haven't been the soul of kindness, but we must draw the line somewhere, mustn't we, Mr. Brough?" Being sick is all very well, but not in the light of day. *(He moves above the stool to left of* **LINGHAM**.*)* For God's sake, let's keep ourselves to ourselves.

**FRANCES** *enters from the kitchen and comes into the living room. She carries a vacuum flask.*

**FRANCES** What is it, Harold? What's the matter?

**LINGHAM** I'm leaving, Mrs. Brough.

**FRANCES** Oh, I'm sorry.

**RICHARD** "We quite understand, but things have gone a bit too far!" The master going through a bad patch is one thing, but off his bloody perch and rolling on the floor like a maniac is another.

**LINGHAM** *(rising and crossing to the door left)* I'll get my things.

**RICHARD** *(sitting in the armchair left centre)* Things!

**FRANCES** *puts the flask on the table and moves centre.*

Yes, get your *little* things – but I've shown you some things that aren't so little.

**FRANCES** Are you going now, Harold – immediately?

**LINGHAM** Yes, I think it's best.

**RICHARD** Yes, go on. Pack up your rubbish, Harold, and get it out of here.

**FRANCES** Shall I call you a taxi?

**RICHARD** Yes, who's going to cart you away?

**LINGHAM** Er, well, Miss Sharp said she'd kindly lend me her van. I'm going to take a room with her sister.

**RICHARD** Well, let's hope her sister's dead, 'cause then she can really keep herself to herself. *(He sees the draughts board on the footstool, snatches it up and flings it across the room to* **LINGHAM**.*)* Here, take your board. Maybe she's got a brother who plays draughts, and if he's sick, let's hope he's decent and doesn't mention it to anyone.

LINGHAM *picks up the board and puts it on the bookshelves left.*

FRANCES Richard, you are being disgusting, and I'm going to tell you something that you don't seem to know. As we're talking of settling accounts, Harold Lingham sank his life savings into your nursing home fees.

RICHARD *(after a pause)* Well, good old Harold. Why don't you two start a sacrifice bureau?

LINGHAM It wasn't anything, really. As you know, I don't have anyone to look after, no family – nothing.

RICHARD Well, don't worry, I won't embarrass you by being grateful or anything like that. *(he pauses)* Well, what are you waiting for? I thought you were leaving.

FRANCES Richard, it's not yet eight o'clock. Before Mr. Lingham leaves, I'm going to give him breakfast. It's a small gesture I'd like to make. Do you mind? *(She moves towards the kitchen.)*

RICHARD Yes, I do mind.

FRANCES *stops and turns.*

Let him feed his face at Elsie's married sister's.

LINGHAM Don't worry about breakfast, Mrs. Brough. I'm really not very hungry. I'll just get my cases.

FRANCES But you can't carry everything.

LINGHAM I'll leave the books and send for them in a few days, if that's not inconvenient to you.

FRANCES Of course not. Do you have a number where I can reach you?

LINGHAM I'm afraid she's not on the phone. I'll drop you a card in a few days. I'll get my cases now.

LINGHAM *stumbles off left.*

FRANCES Are you going to let him go like this? *Are* you?

**RICHARD** *is silent.*

After two years, are you going to let him go like this?

**RICHARD** *is silent.*

**LINGHAM** *enters left, struggling with his hat and overcoat, two suitcases and a holdall. They are obviously heavy and difficult for him to manage. He crosses down centre.*

Oh, please, let me take one of those.

**LINGHAM** Oh, no, really, they are not heavy.

**FRANCES** Please let me help you over to Elsie's.

**LINGHAM** Well, if you're quite sure, that would be nice.

*During the following speech,* **FRANCES** *takes a suitcase and the holdall from* **LINGHAM**, *puts them in the hall, then picks up her bucket bag from the hall, puts it on the table, takes her handbag from the bag and looks in it.* **LINGHAM** *puts the second suitcase on the floor right of the chest down centre, puts his hat on it, closes his overcoat and picks up his hat.*

**RICHARD** Well, Harold, Elsie's hooked you. You're going to be all parcelled up at the nylon shop. Years and years of ham, Harold. It's only the first step, staying with the married sister. It's a lovely day, Harold, let's have a last look at the zoo. One more day with the spotty snakes. Little beauties, weren't they, Harold? *(He rises and moves to left of* **LINGHAM**.*)* That was the day we first pasted pictures in our book. D'you remember, Harold?

**LINGHAM** *(quietly)* Of course, Mr. Brough.

**HENRIETTA**, *unseen by the others, enters on the stairs. She is in her dressing-gown and slippers.*

**RICHARD** *(expansively)* Well, there you are – that's what we need – a day with the snakes. D'you remember how we laughed that day, Harold? Lord, I had to work for that laugh – I nearly burst me braces at the monkey-house, but I had my way, Harold – *(He slaps* LINGHAM *on the back.)* I made you laugh, didn't I, now?

LINGHAM Yes, you did, Mr. Brough.

RICHARD *(leaning on* LINGHAM's *shoulder)* Well, there you are, Leaky-Jugs, and we'll have a day today. We'll tear up the zoo, and your laughter'll ring through the lion-houses and drown the silly beasts' roar. We'll tease all the monkeys, and the tigers'll hide their eyes when they see us coming. We'll stuff our faces with all the chestnuts in London, and we'll give every beggar a penny for his plight. We'll be the lords, Harold, and the beer will flow down to our boots, and we'll come back here and we'll build a fire, and we'll paste the day in our book. *(He releases* LINGHAM.*)* Such a day, Harold – won't that be something?

LINGHAM Yes, it would be, Mr. Brough.

RICHARD *Will* be, Harold, *will* be.

FRANCES Harold's going, Richard.

RICHARD Don't be silly, Frances.

LINGHAM *(after a pause)* I owe you two weeks' rent – *(He takes an envelope from his pocket.)* and six and six for a hyacinth that Mrs. Brough kindly bought.

HENRIETTA *exits up the stairs.*

I will leave the hyacinth behind. Perhaps, Mrs. Brough, you would like it. There are also several books on birds which I should like you to have. I have left them on the table. There's also a shirt of yours which got mixed up with mine in the laundry.

FRANCES *moves to the hall and picks up the holdall.*

I have folded it over the winged armchair; it'll probably need re-ironing. *(He puts the envelope on the table, picks up the suitcase and crosses to the hall.)*

**RICHARD** *is silent.*

Well, good-bye, Mr. Brough. I hope your plans go well. *(He picks up the second suitcase.)*

**FRANCES** *opens the front door.*

**LINGHAM** *and* **FRANCES** *exit by the front door, leaving it open.* **RICHARD** *does not look at them. He stands for a moment, sees the draughts board, picks it up, crosses to the hall and hurls it through the open doorway.*

**RICHARD** *(venomously)* You forgot your board, Leaky-Jugs. What a damn silly thing to call a man.

**RICHARD** *crosses slowly and exits left. After a few moments he re-enters carrying a shirt, a hyacinth and two books. He puts them on the chest down centre and stares at them, then raises his hands and stares at his palms.*

Frances? Frances? *(Anxiety and fear begin to mount in him. With a shout that becomes a scream:)* Frances, those bloody sweats are coming back. Ah, God help me. *(He turns up centre.)*

**FRANCES** *enters by the front door, closes it and moves above the table. She has not heard* **RICHARD** *call.*

**FRANCES** He managed on his own. *(She takes a piece of card and a pencil from the table drawer.)* I'd better put a card in the window. *(She puts the card and pencil on the table.)*

**RICHARD** Card?

**FRANCES** I have to let the room. *(She puts the flask in her bucket bag.)*

**RICHARD** Somebody else? In there?

**FRANCES** Why do you think Harold was – in *there*?

**RICHARD** That was different. Harold was my friend.

**FRANCES** *(crosses to the left-hand fireside seat)* Harold was a lodger, for two pounds, twelve and six. *(She takes a pair of shoes from the seat box.)* It has to be replaced.

**RICHARD** Frances, you can't do that – I didn't mind Harold being in the study.

**FRANCES** *(crossing and putting the shoes on the table)* Well, he's gone.

**RICHARD** *moves to left of* **FRANCES.**

And it's not a study.

**RICHARD** You know what I mean.

**FRANCES** Yes – I know what you mean.

**RICHARD***'s tension, all used up for the moment, has receded, and he begins to apologize.*

**RICHARD** I was silly to shout at Harold like that. I don't know what's the matter with me. I'll fix it up with him. You'll see. I'll fix it up. He'll come trundling back in next to no time. Leaky-Jugs won't stay away for long. *(He moves to the front door.)*

**FRANCES** *puts* **LINGHAM***'s envelope into her handbag.*

**FRANCES** He's gone, Richard, and he took all his miserable bits and pieces that you hate so much with him.

**RICHARD** *(crossing to left of* **FRANCES***)* Frances, what are you talking about?

**FRANCES** *(putting the shoes in her bucket bag)* The organ-grinder's monkey ran away.

**RICHARD** Fran, don't take it so badly. *(charmingly)* Harold knows how I feel about him. *(He tries to convince himself that not too much damage has been done.)* I mean, you can't cancel out a friendship in five minutes' bawling. Like us, Fran, nothing could cancel us out – not our beautiful life.

**FRANCES** *(flatly)* What beautiful life? *(She looks around the room.)*

**RICHARD** *(moving around the room)* I'll do it up, Fran. I'll do it up, you'll see.

**FRANCES** Go ahead.

RICHARD *(moving to left of* FRANCES; *anxiously)* What's the matter?

FRANCES I'm tired, Richard.

> RICHARD *snaps his fingers. The note of feverish excitement comes back into his voice.*

RICHARD *(crossing down left)* Why don't you take the day off, Fran? We could take a Green Line bus somewhere – out – miles out somewhere, where it's green, away from people. That's what you need, Frances, a day out. *(He crosses to her. Pleading:)* Take the day off, Fran.

FRANCES I can't. *(She goes to the hall, collects her raincoat and puts it on.)* One more day off and they'll get rid of me.

RICHARD *(laughing)* Get rid of *you*? No-one could get rid of you. You're irreplaceable.

FRANCES *(moving to right of* RICHARD*)* Every unskilled woman of forty is replaceable, Richard. One more day off and I'm out.

RICHARD *(boisterously)* They need someone to come up there and tell them just what a wonderful woman they've got in you. They don't know how lucky they are. That's it, I'll come right up there and tell them...

FRANCES *(interrupting)* Tell who?

> RICHARD*'s confidence collapses.*

RICHARD Well, whoever these damn stupid idiots are. *(He moves to the stool and sits.)*

FRANCES They don't need me, Richard. I need them.

RICHARD Don't frown, Frances. Don't frown at me. You mustn't take it all so seriously.

FRANCES It is serious. I daren't lose this job.

RICHARD *(irritably)* Why do you keep harping on the job? It's just a temporary thing.

**FRANCES** I've been working on and off for eleven years, since I was twenty-eight. *(She moves above the table.)* I'm thirty-nine – that's hardly temporary.

**RICHARD** Well, I've been sick. I've been sick, Frances.

**FRANCES** I'm not grumbling. *(She collects her scarf from the hall.)* I just said it's not temporary.

**RICHARD** *(rising and moving down centre)* Things are going to change, Frances. We'll toss all those miserable years on the dust-heap in five minutes flat.

**FRANCES** *picks up her bucket bag, goes to the right-hand fireside seat and takes out the raffia work.*

What are you doing?

**FRANCES** Just collecting my things together.

**RICHARD** Stop fussing about. I'm trying to talk to you.

**FRANCES** It'll have to wait.

**RICHARD** Wait? *(His face suddenly lights up excitedly.)* I know – I'll meet you after work. We'll have one of those high teas together. Those teas we used to have. I remember when you could eat eleven scones, Frances.

**FRANCES** *moves to the armchair left centre, sits and puts the raffia into her bucket bag.*

Let's have a really high tea. I bet you can't eat eleven scones anymore.

**FRANCES** *(after a pause; smiling)* Probably not.

**RICHARD** Then I'll meet you at five.

**FRANCES** I can't, Richard. I have early classes tonight. I take a class on Mondays now. I've been doing it for six weeks. Somebody dropped out and they asked me if I'd like to take it over. I only have half an hour to get across London.

**RICHARD** Well, when will I see you?

FRANCES Not till nine. I'll be home about nine. *(She rises, crosses and sits in the armchair above the table.)*

RICHARD *visualises the long day stretching ahead of him.* FRANCES *puts her bag on the table, picks up the pencil and writes on the card.*

RICHARD Nine! That's eleven hours. I can't wait eleven hours, Fran. *Eleven hours.* That's a lifetime. Frances, what shall I do? *(he pauses)* Frances, listen to me. *(He moves to left of* FRANCES.*)* What are you doing?

FRANCES I'm writing a card. I'm advertising the room.

RICHARD *snatches the card and pencil from her.*

RICHARD Here, give it to me. I'll fill it in for you. Wanted, someone to amuse a cripple. It's like Cawley says, isn't it? I'm a blind cripple stumping about in the dark, waiting thirteen hours for my wife to bring home a few pennies. And it's all been eating at you, Frances – *(he spits out the words)* how much you *do* for me.

FRANCES *(wearily)* No, no.

RICHARD The shabby walls are beginning to make you resent me.

FRANCES *(rising)* No, no.

RICHARD Beginning to tell you you've wasted your life in the bus queue for a wash-out.

HENRIETTA *appears on the stairs, still in her dressing-gown.* FRANCES *and* RICHARD *do not see her. She stares down at them, her face the face of a child caught in the agonising despair of divided love. The mask of control is down and her feelings are revealed. The tears pour down her face and we see that she is fully identified with her father's pain. Suddenly people's need has become lovable and weakness something to be cherished. It takes her last vestige of control to remain on the stairs, so she buries her face in her hands.*

FRANCES  No, Richard. It is not like that.

RICHARD  *(crossing to the stool and sitting)* Then what for God's sake is it like?

FRANCES  *(fiddling with her scarf)* Just don't tell me you need my love. My love goes through you like gin. You don't need my love, Richard – it doesn't help. I'm here to hold up the walls, so that you've got a place to cry in – and I don't mind, I only mind when you say the walls are not important.

RICHARD  This *love* – I haven't seen any great show of it.

FRANCES  All right. I betrayed you. I haven't been in love with your dreams. And that's all you care about. Making Ettie's dream of you come true. Well, go ahead and try.

RICHARD  Well, Henrietta's a wonderful girl.

FRANCES  Oh, stop repeating that like a parrot. I'm sick of playing kings and queens, Richard. I'm sick of the bus queues I stand in not being serious. They are serious, Richard. *(A note of hurt and frustration and anger at her inability to keep these words inside herself creeps into her voice.)* And when my back aches, that's serious, too, because my backache brings home seven pounds, fourteen and six. And when I stand in the second queue in the evening, and when I drum handicrafts into the not very bright over-sixteens, that's serious – to the tune of four pounds, twelve and eightpence. I can't give you a crown, Richard.

HENRIETTA *exits up the stairs.*

RICHARD  What happened to the old days, Frances?

FRANCES  They've gone. *(She puts her scarf around her neck.)*

RICHARD  And the story of our love's gone with them?

FRANCES  *(gently)* It was a nice story, Richard – I've lived on it a long time.

RICHARD  *(rising and moving to left of her)* Please, Frances, stay home today. It's so drab in here. I can't stay here today.

FRANCES *(picking up her bags)* I have to go. Your breakfast is on the tray in the kitchen. You'll feel better when you've had some breakfast.

> RICHARD, *almost broken, makes one last desperate attempt to capture her.*

RICHARD If you just stay home today everything will be all right – we could work things out. *(He moves centre.)* That's all we need, Frances, to sit down and straighten things out.

> FRANCES *sits on the bench left of the table.*

If we had one of those picnic lunches, with everything spread out on the floor – one of those lunches where all the jars fall over and everything's a mess... *(He moves to her.)* Don't go, Frances.

FRANCES *(rising and moving above the table)* I'm late, Richard. I'll see you about nine. Henrietta will be down soon. Why don't you talk to her?

RICHARD One day, Frances, that's all I'm asking – one day.

FRANCES *(moving to the front door and opening it)* I have to go.

RICHARD And you want to go.

FRANCES Yes, I do. I'll see you at nine.

> FRANCES *exits by the front door, closing it behind her.* RICHARD *stands for a moment, silent, rubbing the palms of his hands together.*

> HENRIETTA *enters on the stairs. She is wearing the white party dress.* RICHARD *does not see her. He moves to the armchair left centre and picks up his jacket.*

HENRIETTA *(leaning over the banisters)* Father, what are you doing?

RICHARD *(starting)* What? Why are you standing there, Henrietta?

HENRIETTA I was just looking at you.

**RICHARD** *(frowning)* Looking? Oh.

**HENRIETTA** *comes down the stairs and into the room.*

Everyone's gone out, Henrietta. They've all gone out. You'd better go and have your breakfast.

**HENRIETTA** I looked at you for a long time last night. When I came in, you were asleep – and I looked at you. *(She crosses below the stool. Jerkily)* I wanted to tell you I found Soya.

**RICHARD** Oh, yes. *(He puts on his jacket.)*

**HENRIETTA** He was sitting on the wall near his house – he was all hunched up with both thumbs in his mouth – he was crying. His scooter had fallen over into the gutter.

**RICHARD** *(crossing below* **HENRIETTA** *to right of her)* I didn't tell your mother about last night, Henrietta.

**HENRIETTA** *(her speech rushing on)* I didn't speak to Soya, I hid behind a wall – he looked so alone – *(she moves to left of* **RICHARD** *and touches his arm)* there was grease all over his beautiful jacket.

**RICHARD** *(turning to* **HENRIETTA***)* Why are you wearing that dress?

**HENRIETTA** *is not ready to tell him and continues her story.*

**HENRIETTA** Then he jumped down off the wall, and tried to pick up his scooter, but it just lay there. And then he tried again, but he couldn't move it. He hadn't the strength – and he cried out, and ran into the house – and I remembered the night after the Parents' Day when I heard you crying in my room.

*Despite his despair,* **RICHARD***'s feelings are touched.*

**RICHARD** What did you do?

**HENRIETTA** I picked up the scooter. It was quite easy. And then I came home, and looked at you, and as I looked, you shivered.

**RICHARD** Shivered?

**HENRIETTA** You were just cold and I covered you with a blanket and went to bed.

**RICHARD** *(moving to right of the table and picking up his suitcase)* You should go and have your breakfast now, Henrietta.

**HENRIETTA** *(moving above the table)* Where are you going?

**RICHARD** Well, I have – er – one or two things to do. *(He crosses to right of the chest down centre and puts down the case.)*

**HENRIETTA** What things?

**RICHARD** I'm just busy, Henrietta.

**HENRIETTA** *(moving to left of* **RICHARD***)* Where are you going?

**RICHARD** I'm going back to the home.

**HENRIETTA** You can't.

**RICHARD** I should've gone last night. *(He bends and opens the case.)*

**HENRIETTA** You can't go back to the home – I know what they'll do to you.

**RICHARD** *(wearily)* They can't do anything to me, Henrietta. There's nothing left. All my energy has been squeezed up and spitted out.

**HENRIETTA** You can't go back to the home.

**RICHARD** I've crawled around in a pit all my life, Henrietta. I've clutched at the walls and they've crumbled away in my hands – it's all fallen in on me, Henrietta – Frances is in the bus with her little bag clutched up in her hand, and Harold's gone – he found that birds and flowers are not enough – I wish it *were* enough. *(He takes the books from the chest, puts them in the case and closes it.)* I wish I were an old man and could make do with a hyacinth.

**HENRIETTA** *(softly)* What about me?

**RICHARD** *turns his head away from her.*

RICHARD Somewhere in my darkness I heard you sing, and you thought I answered with an ugly call – somewhere I clutched at your life in the wrong way, Henrietta, and now I have to go away.

HENRIETTA But what about me?

RICHARD You'll be all right, Henrietta. *(He picks up the case and crosses towards the hall.)*

HENRIETTA *shakes her head.*

HENRIETTA *(running to left of the stool)* I'll never have a party. Without you, I'll never have a party.

RICHARD I can't stay, Henrietta.

HENRIETTA But the party was for you – it was always for you. I didn't know until last night, but all the months when you were away, I'd been planning it for now – it must be now. *(She runs to the window up left and closes the curtains.)*

RICHARD Henrietta – it's eight o'clock in the morning.

HENRIETTA *(running to the curtains up right centre and closing them)* I know it's a silly time to have a party, but I've drawn the curtains. *(She runs to the shelves left and switches on the candles.)* Then we can switch on the lanterns – I could never decide about the colours. *(She moves to the fireplace and switches on the lanterns over it.)* Pink is lovely – but green is more eerie. *(She crosses and switches on the hall lantern, then crosses and pushes the armchair left centre down stage. Tremulously, for fear of breaking the mood:)* First, you must sit here. *(She crosses to* RICHARD.*)*

RICHARD *puts down the case.*

*(She leads* RICHARD *to the armchair.)* Where everyone can see you.

RICHARD *sits in the armchair.*

Now. *(She switches on the lantern on the chest down centre.)* There! I can see you – I can see you so clearly. Now wait, and

I will bring in the food. *(She runs to the kitchen door.)* There are all sorts of heavenly bits and pieces.

HENRIETTA *exits to the kitchen.* RICHARD *rises and moves to left of the fireplace, a dark part of the room.*

HENRIETTA *enters from the kitchen carrying a tray of savouries. She stands in the hall looking for* RICHARD.

Father?

RICHARD *(from the shadows; quietly)* Yes?

HENRIETTA *(crossing to right of* RICHARD*)* Which would you like? These are salty, and those are sweet, but that one has a little almond. But you must choose.

RICHARD *(unresponsively)* I don't know, Henrietta.

HENRIETTA *(desperately)* Then I'll decide. You close your eyes. *(She leads* RICHARD *down centre.)* But come into the light – I can't find your face. Now close your eyes and open your mouth.

RICHARD *closes his eyes.*

*(She puts a small savoury into* RICHARD*'s mouth. Suddenly:)* Oh, I'd forgotten about the rose. *(She puts the tray on the stool, goes to the right-hand fireside seat and takes the red rose from the seat box.)* Elsie couldn't decide where I should wear it. Isn't it beautiful?

RICHARD *stares at the rose.*

I know, you should wear it. *(She puts the rose in* RICHARD*'s lapel.)*

RICHARD *touches the rose.*

It's perfect. How funny, I never thought of it before. *(She takes* RICHARD*'s arm and leads him to the armchair.)* Oh, I wish – I wish Mother could have been here, and Soya and Elsie, and Harold – and – old Mrs. Pleasance, and Alison Verney and Jean Anderson, and Paula Wright –

RICHARD *sits in the armchair.*

and Elizabeth Preeney, and Penelope Saunders – and Soya's
father, and Soya's mother – and the law partners, and the
ex-vicar, and Dr Cawley, and old Nurse Robot, and Elsie's
Mr. Vinegar. But no-one is coming, and I want so much to
say: this is my father. This is Paula Wright and Alison Verney.
He must tell you the story of the bears – I've never been able
to describe it – *(she kneels right of* RICHARD*)* how they fell
in their tea cups, and their paws were covered with sugar,
and they rubbed it all over their faces – *(She rises and turns
away centre.)* Father's bears have such large tea cups, larger
than any other bears in the world. When he looks in shop
windows, the feathers in hats stand up higher.

RICHARD *smiles.*

And eggs jump out of their shells. *(She kneels beside* RICHARD.*)*
There's Ann Metcalf and Elizabeth Preeney. *(she rises)* This is
my father – who can talk to crocodiles in their own crocodilian
language. He knows them so well they allow him to count
their teeth in a terribly intimate way –

*She begins to catch the mood of* RICHARD*'s softening
behaviour, and begins to enjoy the fantasy which she is
creating for him.*

then he claps his hands and they slink away into the water –
*(with mock fear)* terribly, terribly afraid.

RICHARD *laughs.*

Yes, this is my father. I've never told you much about him –
*(She moves behind the armchair left centre.)* but horses resent
their blinkers when they see him coming, and policemen feel
foolish and drop down their hands and stand with their mouths
drooping open.

RICHARD *is now fully enjoying the game.*

*(she crosses to centre and looks at* RICHARD*)* This is my
father. When he smiles up at little houses, lights go on in

their windows, and puppies stop crying in their cages, and dusty old gentlemen with stuffy moustaches, hide their heads in their briefcases when he winks his eye – and – and...

**RICHARD** And it's only known in very secret places why he feels like a king – it's because he has such a wonderful daughter.

**HENRIETTA** And sometimes he's happy, and sometimes he drinks, and sometimes he cries in the night – a beautiful cry that really shows he's somebody. *(She throws herself into* **RICHARD***'s arms.)*

**RICHARD** Won't you be frightened when the little lights go out?

**HENRIETTA** Will there ever be anything beautiful again?

**RICHARD** We'll try, Henrietta, we'll try.

*Curtain.*

# FURNITURE AND PROPERTY LIST

## ACT I

### Scene One

*On stage:* Table. *In drawer:* party list, pencil, card
2 benches
Upright armchair
Sofa. *On it:* cushion
Combined stool and steps
Fireside seat right. *In it:* polythene bag of raffia work,
bundles of coloured raffia
Fireside seat left. *In it:* pair of shoes
Chest (down centre)
Armchair (left centre)
Footstool (above armchair left centre)
Built-in shelves (left)　　*In them:* books
　　　　　　　　　　　　　*On lower shelf:* telephone with
　　　　　　　　　　　　　　　long lead
*On mantelpiece:* blue vase, party list, memoranda
book, hand-bell
Chintz window curtains

*On walls:* floral prints
*On stairs:* linoleum
*On floor of room:* carpet
*In hall:* runner
*On windowsills:* vases of flowers
Fire-screen
Electric wall brackets
Electric pendant in hall
Light switches at foot of stairs
Clockwork door bell on front door
Coat hooks in hall

Doors closed
    Windows closed

Window curtains open
    Light fittings on

*Offstage:* String bag. *In it:* shopping (Frances)
    Bucket bag. *In it:* 2 office files, typing paper, vacuum
      flask (Frances)
    Tray. *On it:* 3 plates, 3 small knives, 3 raffia mats, 3
      paper serviettes, tablecloth (Frances)
    Dress box. *In it:* white dress (Lingham)
    Laundry box with laundry (Lingham)
    Tray. *On it:* 3 cups, 3 saucers, 3 teaspoons, pot of tea,
      jug of milk, bowl of lump sugar, plate of crumpets
      (Frances)

*Personal:* Frances: handbag. *In it:* letter

**Scene Two**

*Strike:* Everything from table
    Bucket bag from hall
    Laundry from hall
    Frances' coat and scarf from hall
    Frances' gloves and handbag from bench
    Dress, dress box, etc.

Move stool to up left of chest

Move armchair to up left of stool

Set:        *On stool:* draughts board and draughts men
               *Beside telephone:* box for draughts men

Doors closed

Windows closed

Window curtains closed

Light fittings on

*Offstage:*    Box with artificial roses (Elsie)
               Bucket bag with raffia work (Frances)

*Personal:*   Soya: crash helmet

### Scene Three

*Strike:*      Frances' handbag, bucket bag, coat and gloves
               Books from shelves left
               Rose from chest

Replace armchair left centre to original position

Move stool to fire place and open out as steps

*Set:*         *Over fireplace:* Chinese lanterns (lit)
               *On shelves* left: small decorative candles (lit)
               *On chest:* lantern (lit)
               *On sofa:* lantern (unlit)
               *On table:* memoranda book and bell from mantelpiece

Doors closed

Windows closed

Window curtains closed

Light fittings on

Lanterns on

Candles on

*Offstage:*    3 packets of biscuits (Henrietta)
               Suitcase (Richard)

Bottle of gin (Richard)
Pair of long white gloves (Frances)
Pair of long ivory gloves (Elsie)
3 glasses (Richard)

*Personal:* Lingham: watch

## ACT II

### Scene One

*Strike:* Suitcase
White gloves

*Set:* Telephone on bookshelves
*On footstool:* draughts box and board
*On mantelpiece:* bell and memorandum book
*On table:* Gin bottle with cap on, 2 glasses
*In table drawer:* party list
*In hall:* bucket bag with office files and Frances'
handbag
*On hall hooks:* Richard's hat and coat, Lingham's hat
and coat, Frances' scarf and coat with gloves in
pocket, Elsie's wrap
*In right-hand fireside seat:* raffia work, red rose

Kitchen door open

Other doors closed

Windows closed

Window curtains closed

Light fittings on

Lanterns out

Candles out

*Offstage:* Tray. *On it:* traycloth, plate with meat, knife, fork,
cup, saucer, spoon, coffee-pot (Elsie)
Suitcase (Richard)

## Scene Two

*Strike:*     Glasses from table

*Set:*        *On sofa:* rug
            *On footstool:* draught board
            *On floor beside sofa:* empty gin bottle
            *On back of armchair:* Richard's jacket

All doors closed

Window curtains closed

Windows closed

Light fittings on

Lanterns out

Candles out

*Offstage:*   Glass of Alka-Seltzer (Richard)
           Vacuum flask (Frances)
           2 suitcases (Lingham)
           Holdall (Lingham)
           Shirt (Richard)
           2 books (Richard)
           Hyacinth (Richard)
           Tray of savouries (Henrietta)

*Personal:*   Lingham: envelope

## LIGHTING PLOT

Property fittings required: electric wall brackets, hall pendant, Chinese lanterns, small candles

Interior. A living room and hall. The same scene throughout

The Main Acting Areas are centre, at an armchair left centre, at a sofa up right centre, at a bench right and in the hall up right

The Apparent Sources of Light are, in daytime, windows up right centre and up left centre; and at night, wall-brackets right and left and an electric pendant in the hall.

**ACT I, Scene One**. Late afternoon in early spring

*To open:* Fittings on
*Sunset effect outside windows*

*Cue* 1    **Lingham** enters by front door
*Cross-fade exterior lights for night
    effect.*

**ACT I, Scene Two**. Night

*To open:* Lights as at the end of the previous Scene

*No cues*

**ACT I, Scene Three**. Night

*To open:* Lights as at the end of the previous Scene
Lanterns up centre, lit
Candles left, lit
Lantern down centre, lit

*Cue* 2    **Henrietta** switches off lights
*Snap out fittings.*
*Snap out covering lights.*

*Cue* 3    **Henrietta** switches on lights
*Snap in fittings.*
*Snap in covering lights.*

**ACT II, Scene One**. Night

*To open:* Lights as at the end of the previous Scene
Lanterns up centre, out
Candles, out
Lantern down centre, out

*No cues*

**ACT II, Scene Two**. Early morning

*To open:* Daylight effect outside windows
Fittings on
Lanterns and candles out

*Cue 4*  **Frances** opens curtains up right centre
*Bring up onstage lights right centre.*

*Cue 5*  **Frances** opens curtains up left
*Bring up onstage lights left.*

*Cue 6*  **Frances** switches out light
*Snap out fittings.*

*Cue 7*  **Henrietta** closes curtains up left
*Reduce onstage lights left.*

*Cue 8*  **Henrietta** closes curtains up right
centre
*Reduce onstage lights right centre.*

*Cue 9*  **Henrietta** switches on candles
*Snap in candles left.*

*Cue 10*  **Henrietta** switches on lanterns up
centre
*Snap in lanterns up centre.*

*Cue 11*  **Henrietta** switches on hall lantern
*Snap in hall lantern.*

*Cue 12*  **Henrietta** switches on lantern down
centre
*Snap in lantern down centre.*

## EFFECTS PLOT

**ACT I, Scene One**. *No cues*

**ACT I, Scene Two**. *No cues*

**ACT I, Scene Three**. *No cues*

**ACT II, Scene One**. *Cue 1*

      **Richard** "...with me around."

      *Telephone rings.*

**ACT II, Scene Two**. *No cues*

* 9 7 8 0 5 7 3 0 1 3 3 0 0 *